READ ME.

READ ME.

Roger Horberry & Gyles Lingwood

10
Lessons
for Writing
Great Copy

Laurence King Publishing

Published in 2014
by Laurence King Publishing Ltd
361–373 City Road
London EC1V 1LR
Tel +44 20 7841 6900
Fax +44 20 7841 6910
enquiries@laurenceking.com
www.laurenceking.com

A catalog record for this book is available from the
British Library

ISBN 978 1 78067 3486

Design: Two Sheds Design
Senior Editor: Peter Jones

Printed in China

Contents

Does the world *really* need another book on copywriting?

Aren't bookstores around the globe already suitably stocked with similar stuff? Obviously we're biased, but we think the answers to those questions are "yes" and "no"—in that order. Allow us to explain.

Many books on copywriting tell it like it ought to be, not like it is. In contrast, *Read Me* combines tried-and-tested techniques, practical knowledge, and hands-on exercises that reflect the rough and tumble of real-world copywriting. It's the book we wanted when we were starting out, but couldn't find because it wasn't available. Now, decades later, we're in the happy position of being able to share what we've learned from over 20 years each at the creative coalface. *Read Me* is the result.

For added oomph we've included contributions from some highly accomplished US and UK writers working in advertising, branding, design, and beyond. Their brief was simple: "What pearls of wisdom would you pass on to a cub copywriter or the young you?" The idea is to let you pick the brains of top practitioners working in a variety of areas who share many of the challenges copywriters face. No group has a monopoly on knowledge, and by sharing we all benefit.

Who this book is for

The short answer to this is anyone who uses words to engage and persuade their readers. The longer answer is anyone who works—or hopes to work—in advertising, design, branding, communications, PR, marketing, sales, or management. You might be a student looking for job-specific skills; you might be a teacher or trainer looking for course material. All brothers and sisters of the word are welcome here.

How it works

This book takes the form of ten self-contained lessons, each covering a subject or idea we believe copywriters need to know. Because these lessons are pretty modular you can read them in any order without suffering undue psychological damage, although starting at the beginning and working through to the end is probably your best bet.

We've made each lesson as practical as possible, so when we cover a slightly abstract subject like "audience" or "brand" we do it in a way that emphasizes "audiences *and writing*", "brands *and writing*," and so on. Absorbing and acting on this information will give your career a rocket-assisted launch and dramatically improve your understanding of how this business works.

Most of the lessons end with one or more workouts designed to sharpen your skills. We encourage you, urge you, *beg* you to have a go at these. The only way to improve at anything is to push yourself beyond where you feel comfortable, and by putting what you've read into practice you'll get so much more from it. Best of all, you can upload your words to the workout area of this book's website at www.readmewriting.com and see how others have responded to these challenges.

Why we've written it

Our main aim is to describe the art and craft of copywriting and the key skills you'll need to succeed in this competitive but incredibly satisfying career. We also explore an underappreciated theme in contemporary copywriting—a theme we've christened "brandwriting." Put all that together and this book is our take on what it means to write for—and about—brands in the twenty-first century.

How it came about

Read Me grew out of a series of lectures we developed for undergraduates taking the BA (Hons) Creative Advertising degree at the University of Lincoln in the UK. These, in turn, grew out of our individual research into important industry issues. Our approach reflects what Gyles and his academic colleagues describe as "research-informed teaching." Much of our material— particularly the exercises at the end of each lesson— has been repeatedly tested in front of Lincoln's advertising undergraduates, so as well as being a resource for copywriters, this book is also a ready-made professional writing course for trainers and teachers in industry and academia.

The important point is that each lesson reflects our conversations with industry figures and answers the real-world needs of students and junior writers. That's what we mean when we describe a particular technique as "tried and tested." We're confident these

approaches work for the simple reason they've repeatedly been shown to do so in both the classroom and the creative studio.

Lastly but not leastly, this book is the lovechild of Gyles and Roger working together in perfect harmony. That's why we've written it in the third person plural—"we," "us," and so on. For the most part it describes our shared understanding, so this approach makes perfect sense. Here and there we need to write from an individual perspective, which means switching to the first person —"I," "me," and the like. Just think of *Read Me* as our combined opinion and you won't go far wrong.

Lesson One:
The Big Picture

Our kind of copywriting

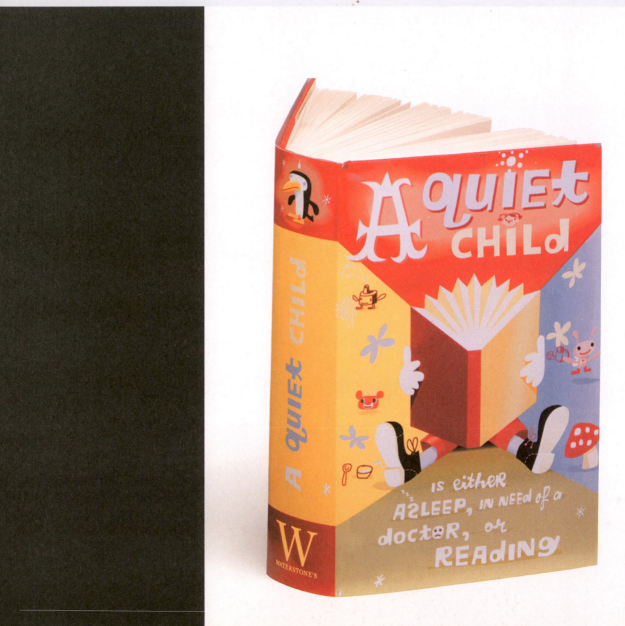

Writing matters, but then we would say that, wouldn't we?

In this lesson we describe our take on writing today, we define the writer's job, and we suggest a manifesto for our kind of copywriting. It's the foundation on which the rest of this book is built, so read this first and what follows will make more sense.

It's sometimes said the world is "post words." If that's true then copywriting belongs in the past, along with other quaint relics of yesteryear, like quilt making, folk dancing, or marrying one's close cousins.

"Post words" is an intriguing idea spoiled only by the inconvenient fact that it's complete and utter rubbish. It suggests people no longer read or respect the written word, which clearly isn't the case. As proof, consider J. K. Rowling's bulging bank balance, Amazon's stratospheric Kindle sales, the army of local people fighting to keep neighborhood libraries open, and the social media-enabled multitude whose words have, on occasion, helped changed the world.

Yes, attention spans are shorter and yes, there are shiny new forms of media competing for our attention, but let's not get carried away. People still read, they just do it in more and different ways. With apologies to Mark Twain, rumours of writing's death are greatly exaggerated.

"Ah," say the naysayers, "surely you know we live in a visual culture where a picture is worth a thousand words?" And that's fine, but some problems don't lend themselves to pictorial solutions. Find us an image that absolutely and unambiguously says, "Just do it," or "Buy it. Sell it. Love it," or "Solutions for a small planet," or "Because I'm worth it," or "Impossible is nothing," or… well, you get the idea.[1] We're certainly not suggesting words have any priority over images; our point is both have their place. A picture may well be worth a thousand words, but just try making that very point with a picture alone.

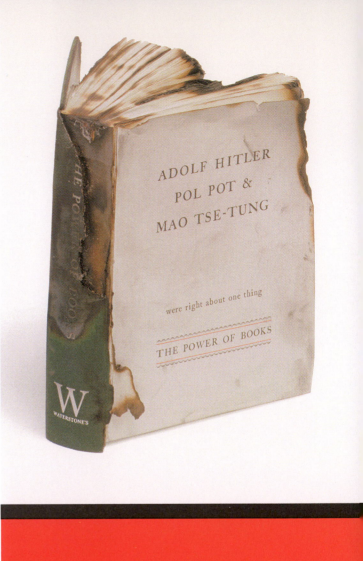

A poster should contain no more than eight words, which is the maximum the average reader can take at a single glance. This, however, is for Economist readers.

The Economist.

top: Elegant, intelligent ads for UK bookseller Waterstones that celebrate reading and the power of the written word.

above: One of many brilliant text-only ads for *The Economist*. The self-referential subject of this example is an added bonus.

This message from Olympus is about adventure and attitude, a combination almost impossible to convey using imagery alone. Why else do you think they wrote all those words?

1. Taglines for Nike, eBay, IBM, L'Oréal, and Adidas, in case you were wondering.

At last, a camera for anyone who's ever said, "I'm going to get a picture of the inside of that shark's mouth if it's the last thing I do".

Time was you'd be afraid to take a compact digital camera to the beach, much less into the water. You'd be terrified to drop it, throw it, dunk it, or kick it. Now you can do all of those things without a care in the world.

Because this is one tough camera. The sleek, solid, Olympus Mju 790 SW, with 7.1 megapixels, 3X optical zoom, Face Detection and 23 scene modes (including four underwater) is the perfect companion in just about any photographic situation. We call it the Olympus Tough. It's waterproof to a depth of three metres, shockproof to 1.5 metres, and it's even freezeproof to minus ten degrees. But quite apart from its robustness, it's also very good-looking. It's neat, stylish, and comes in four colours – starry silver, midnight black, sunset orange or marine blue. So, the sooner you've braved the forbidding terrains of Jessops, Boots, John Lewis or any good photographic store, the sooner you can start taking pictures of things you were never able to take pictures of before. In places you were never able to take pictures in before. And, should you ever find that Death actually is staring you in the face, at least you can ask Him to say cheese.

The Olympus Tough can take it.

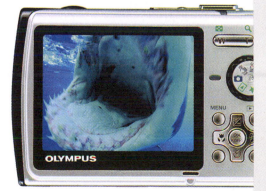

OK, so perhaps people read...

...but they don't read *copy*, do they? Again we must disagree. People will read what copywriters produce for precisely as long as it interests them, informs them, or suggests a benefit. As proof, look around at the acres of excellent copy being produced for design, brands, digital, packaging, and marketing in general. Someone must be reading and reacting to all those words or no sane organization would commission and pay for them. Despite what the skeptics may tell you, first-class copy is being produced and consumed with as much enthusiasm as ever.

OK, OK, so people read, and perhaps they even read copy...

...but not *long* copy surely? For long copy—which we'll define as anything over around 100 words—is, by common consent, long dead. And it's true; ads featuring hundreds of carefully crafted words are no more. During the 1990s the long-copy ad somehow ceased to be, and the occasional examples we see today tend to be pastiches of past forms.

But here's the thing: *Who says long copy has to go on ads?* The marketing mix is broad—long copy is alive and well and living on websites, brochures, packaging, and so on. It's not clear how this rather obvious truth has escaped general detection. In fact we reject the whole long-copy/short-copy debate as largely irrelevant; in the end all that matters is the effect a piece of communication produces, not the number of characters it contains. All of which leads us nicely into our next point—the sort of copywriting we're talking about and the sort of writer we've written this book for.

Check out the nouns—"a drizzle of olive oil," "a scatter of wild bay leaves." Packaging is home to some of the best copywriting around.

Ever found yourself absentmindedly consuming the words on the back of a cereal box as you absentmindedly consume its contents? Same idea here.

Carton 1

Yellow

Bendy

the soul of a fruit

So, you thought a good banana was easily recognisable? Yellow, bendy, no big bruises? Maybe so, but can you see into the banana's soul? We believe we can. It's a gift that was given to us at a fairground long ago. And it's why we work with the Rainforest Alliance, who employ great people like Carlos. His job is to check all our bananas have been grown with respect for local biodiversity, by farms who protect the surrounding rainforests and by farmers who are treated and paid fairly for their work. Oh yes. Those bananas have got soul.

No big bruises

Soul

fancy a chat?

Us too. Just pop in to Fruit Towers, 1 Goldhawk Estate, Brackenbury Road, London, W6 0BA or ring the banana phone on 020 8600 3993. In Ireland, visit us at Fruit Towers, 46 Mountjoy Square, Dublin 1 or call 01 864 4100. Otherwise email doormat@innocentdrinks.com, or even join the family at www.innocentdrinks.com/family

PROTECTS WHAT'S GOOD
Tetra Pak

Carton 2

pounds of fruit

Hard maths – simultaneous quadratic equations, advanced trigonometry and getting stabbed with a compass.

Simple maths – this carton of smoothie is better value than the sum of buying all the fruit yourself, making it at home and then having to do the washing up afterwards.

For those of you who like equations, here's one for you:

$$f + b + w = z$$
$$i = a$$

key:
f = cost of fruit z = less value
b = blender hunt i = innocent carton
w = wrinkly hands a = better value

For those of you who are more visual types, here's a nice picture to illustrate:

or

And for those of you who like small dogs in jumpers, this one's for you:

fancy a chat?

Us too. Just pop in to Fruit Towers, 1 Goldhawk Estate, Brackenbury Road, London, W6 0BA or ring the banana phone on 020 8600 3993. In Ireland, visit us at Fruit Towers, 46 Mountjoy Square, Dublin 1 or call 01 864 4100. Otherwise email doormat@innocentdrinks.com, or even join the family at www.innocentdrinks.com/family

PROTECTS WHAT'S GOOD
Tetra Pak

Carton 3

The Cosa Nostra

There's a reason why this recipe tastes so very good. And it's a big fat secret. But since you asked...we're very specific about the mangoes we use and the exact moment when they're ripe enough to crush. A day either way is a day too wrong. But our growers have signed special forms. They've sworn an oath. We'll never tell and neither will they. So trust us, these secrets are for your drinking benefit. Don't try to find out too much; accidents will happen. Capiche?

fancy a chat?

Us too. Just pop in to Fruit Towers, 1 Goldhawk Estate, Brackenbury Road, London, W6 0BA or ring the banana phone on 020 8600 3993. In Ireland, visit us at Fruit Towers, 46 Mountjoy Square, Dublin 1 or call 01 864 4100. Otherwise email doormat@innocentdrinks.com, or even join the family at www.innocentdrinks.com/family

PROTECTS WHAT'S GOOD
Tetra Pak

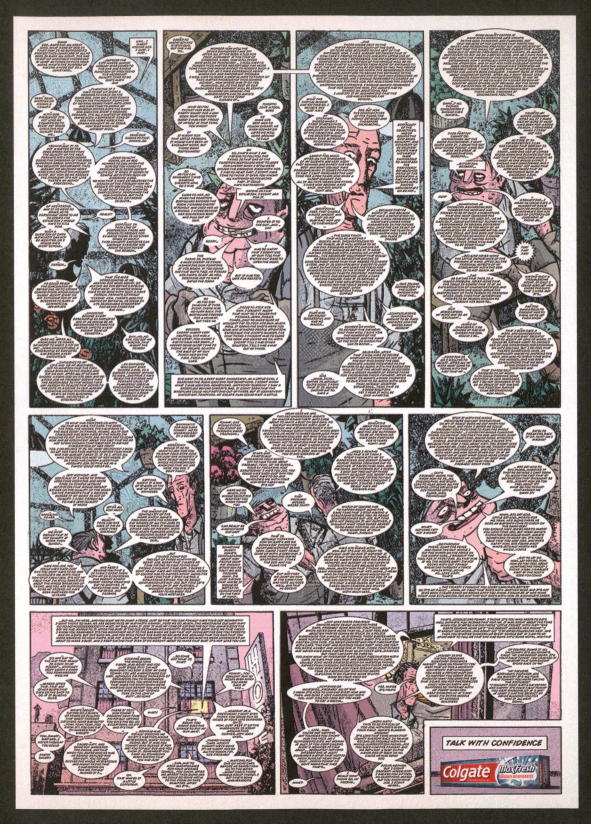

It's a long-copy ad all right, but the words aren't there to be read.

Ironically the one place where copy really *has* fallen out of favor is advertising, the industry that invented copywriting in the first place.

Why so? Partly it's about skills. It's been suggested that many of today's ad copywriters "will never write what we've known as a headline outside of an advertising class," while according to a 2010 study by the UK firm, Think Eye Tracking, a competition-winning long-copy ad from 2010 scored lower for eye tracking, engagement, and recall than a similar piece from 1999, leading the study's authors to ask, "Have agencies forgotten how to do long copy?"

Partly it's about client pressure. Veteran UK copywriter Neil French comments, "How many times have you been in a client meeting, and he's announced 'People don't read copy any more'. This coming from a man with a newspaper poking out of his briefcase. And if you point this out, he says, 'Well, I do, of course. But the public doesn't.'"

Partly it's because international campaigns demand international solutions. According to Mr. Bean creator Richard Curtis, one of the reasons the movies succeed everywhere on earth is their lack of language. When Mr. Bean needs a new pair of underpants he doesn't head to a store with a sign saying "Haberdashers," he heads to a store with a giant pair of Y-fronts hanging outside. We get it, whatever language we speak.

But mainly it seems to be a combination of changing creative trends and the advent of new technologies. Copy, when it features in the mix, doesn't mean headlines and body text. Instead it's woven into visuals, products, apps, and experiences that play out across multiple platforms and in multiple locations. As a result, today's advertising copywriters tend to produce relatively few actual words. Funny old world, isn't it?

John Simmons

You make your own way. It might not be a fast or a dynamic way but you'll get somewhere eventually. That's OK. All I can say is take what life throws at you. You'll learn from it and you'll use it. Never get bitter, don't give in to disappointment. You'll find that every experience is a step along the way to being a writer—as long as that's the path you've decided to head along. You might find it's a meandering path, and there probably are shortcuts if you're lucky. What matters is to commit yourself to going down that path, and to carry on even when it seems to be leading nowhere. I never found the shortcuts, but I think you enjoy the journey in the end.

John was formerly Director of Verbal Identity at Interbrand in London, and is now an independent writer. John writes for companies and brands in the UK and overseas, and runs highly regarded workshops with www.dark-angels.org.uk. His many books include *We, Me, Them & It, Dark Angels, The Invisible Grail*, and *26 Ways of Looking at a Blackberry*. John also co-edited *The Economist Guide to Brands and Branding*, wrote a regular column about brands in *The Observer*, and is co-author of *Room 121*. As he might say, blimey!

Various Artists is a new creative agency. We don't do this or this, but we do make you feel like this, this, this and this. We're great if you want to feel more like this, or like this, or even like that, but we'll never make you feel like this or this. And definitely not like that. This? Sure. This? Naturally. This? Comes as standard. Hey, if you want to feel like this we'll do it. We're all grown ups. But we try and stay away from this. That's just too far. If you'd like to see some of our work or find out more, you can use this, this, or this.

Various Artists'   +44 (0)161 637 1125 hello@byvariousartists.com

How do you get across on a business card that you strive to uncover the big ideas, push for the great concepts, work hard for success, thrive on exploring the world, want to learn about everything and anything, live for the summer, can't get enough of music festivals but ultimately, just really love writing copy?

Olly Copywriter
ollycooper.com

ollycooper@hotmail.co.uk
07810774749

Words aren't fussy, they'll work wherever you put them, from websites (top) and business cards (above) to storefronts (opposite). "Everything is media," according to TBWA bigwig Lee Clow. You can see his point.

Official Notice: The Proprietor is hereby licensed to sell items including, but not limited to: Malodorous Gases, Children's Ears, Gore, Fear (Tinned only), Pencils, and other items as specified in the Monster Retailer's Act of 1827, Clause 14, Subsection 5, Revision (b).

Hoxton Street Monster Supplies

ESTD 1818

~ Bespoke and Everyday Items for the Living, Dead and Undead ~

ONLY ONE
"GIANT
IN THE SHOP
AT A TIME

CUSTOMERS
ARE POLITELY
REQUESTED
TO REFRAIN
FROM EATING
THE STAFF

NOCTURNAL
OPENING
(BY APPOINTMENT)
FOR VAMPIRE
CUSTOMERS
ONLY

BEANS
(MAGIC OR
OTHERWISE)
ARE NOT
ACCEPTED
AS PAYMENT

HUMANS
WELCOME,
BUT ENTIRELY
AT THEIR
OWN RISK

ANGRY MOBS
PLEASE DOUSE
YOUR TORCHES
BEFORE ENTERING
THE SHOP

Meet the brandwriter

Allow us to propose a new profession—brandwriting—and a new professional, the brandwriter.

You won't be surprised to hear a brandwriter is a copywriter who creates words for brands. Those words can appear pretty much anywhere a brand wishes to communicate. Packaging copy for breakfast cereal? Brandwriting. Web text for an online store? Same again. Brochure for a charity? Script for a corporate video? Flyer for a launch event? Presentation for senior managers? Program for a music festival? All 100 percent brandwriting.

What brandwriting *doesn't* mean is advertising, at least not the variety practiced by mainstream agencies. As we've mentioned, the advertising copywriter's remit has expanded to the point where words are just one weapon in their arsenal. This move to the visual/conceptual is exciting stuff (indeed it's been called "the new creative revolution") but our concern here is with words, primarily for print and screen. We don't discuss the very particular skills needed to write for TV, radio, outdoor, and so on (although some of our contributors have wise words to say on these subjects), we're not concerned with experiences or environments, nor do we talk about ad agency-specific activities like strategy or planning. If that's wrong, we don't want to be right.

Perhaps the biggest difference between advertising copywriters and brandwriters is the volume of words they produce. Many contemporary ads are about bringing a single killer concept to life in as few words as possible. In contrast, brandwriting is very much about words and the articulation of complex ideas in the most engaging, persuasive way possible. Although related, these two approaches are very different.

Having said all that, a quick flick ahead will show you we've used the term "copywriter" instead of "brandwriter" throughout this book. That's because the world calls what we do "copywriting," so it makes sense to play along, even if the label isn't quite right. Just bear in mind that writing for brands in all their many and varied forms is what *Read Me* is about, and if you choose to call what you do "brandwriting," that's fine by us.

How to Write a Manifesto

Today, we write a manifesto.

Today, our second sentence starts with the first word of the first sentence.

We write a short sentence.

Then a shorter one.

Then a really, really long one that maybe doesn't make any sense but is immediately followed by

One.

Word.

Sentences.

Then we make our point even clearer

By using fragmented prepositional phrases.

By repeating that first preposition.

By doing it a total of three times.

And then we have another really long sentence that builds up excitement for our overarching concept that is summed up in a word that makes absolutely no sense.

Kumquat.

A great take on manifestos from New York copywriter and creative director Kim Mok.

This Red Brick Beer packaging by advertising agency 22squared is proof—if it were needed —that long copy is alive and well. It doesn't just live in ad land anymore.

One more thing before we begin

A number of themes come up again and again in this book; they add up to what we must self-consciously call our "manifesto." So allow us to introduce a series of truths we hold to be self-evident.

We believe...

...Craft is key

Copywriting is a career for doers not talkers. Being a doer means developing your hands-on writing skills; it's essential you can sit down, tune in, and turn out appealing, effective text ranging from a three-word slogan to a three-thousand-word article at absurdly short notice. Amid all the noise and nonsense of modern life it's good to have something as solid as a craft skill to fall back on. Getting your hands dirty doing stuff in this way is ever so slightly noble. OK, it's not the same as being a fire fighter in the heroic occupation stakes, but the ability to create something out of nothing can be profoundly satisfying, and is one of the principal rewards of the job.

...Words are ideas (and vice versa)

All copywriters are in the ideas business—that's because words are ideas in another form. The process of identifying and improving promising ideas is the starting point for the whole writing process. The act of getting something down on paper or screen forces the copywriter to explore the limits of an idea, test its integrity, and fix any problems they find. It's about *getting the thinking right*. We can't overemphasize the importance of this process—if a piece of copy isn't conceptually robust, then the chances are it won't work because readers will sense its shortcomings and respond accordingly. Get the thinking right and whatever follows has at least a fighting chance of success.

...Copy is conversation (and vice versa)

Good copywriting tends to read like one person talking to another. This conversational approach has become even more important with the rise of digital. In the analog past, copywriting was a one-way street— copywriters sweated over high-impact headlines and beautifully wrought body copy that delivered a nicely packaged message to readers, with little or no

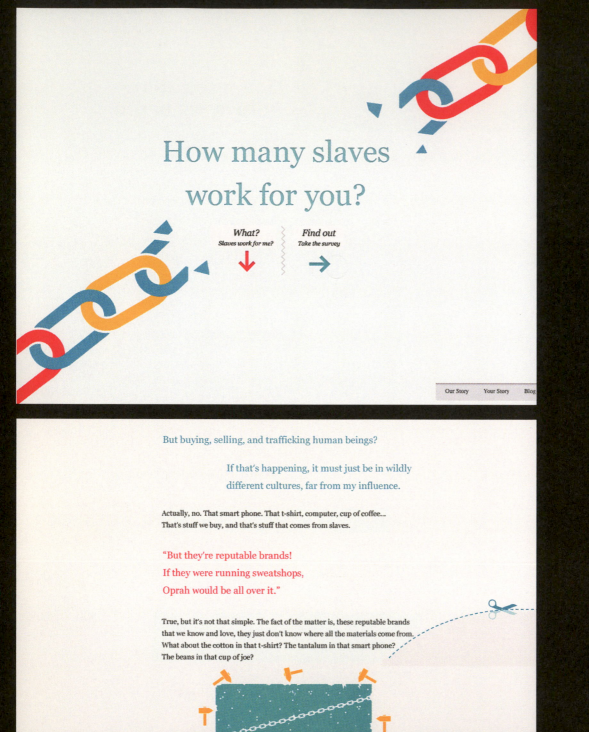

How many slaves work for you?

What?
Slaves work for me?
↓

Find out
Take the survey
→

Our Story   Your Story   Blog

But buying, selling, and trafficking human beings?

If that's happening, it must just be in wildly
different cultures, far from my influence.

Actually, no. That smart phone. That t-shirt, computer, cup of coffee...
That's stuff we buy, and that's stuff that comes from slaves.

"But they're reputable brands!
If they were running sweatshops,
Oprah would be all over it."

True, but it's not that simple. The fact of the matter is, these reputable brands
that we know and love, they just don't know where all the materials come from.
What about the cotton in that t-shirt? The tantalum in that smart phone?
The beans in that cup of joe?

Dialogue-based copy for the anti-slavery
website slaveryfootprint.org. The relaxed,
conversational tone makes the subject
matter all the more shocking.

The copy here tells a quirky story about the product, but what it's *really* doing is building the brand's personality. The gag about corners is priceless.

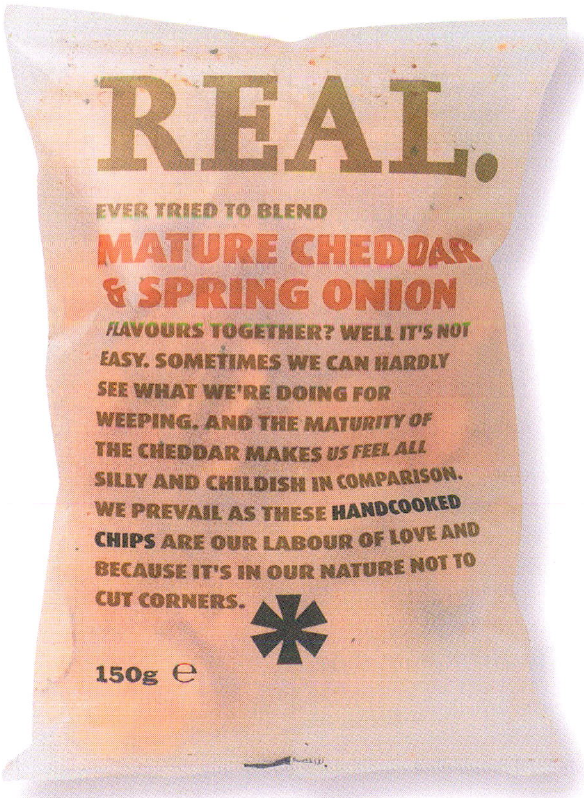

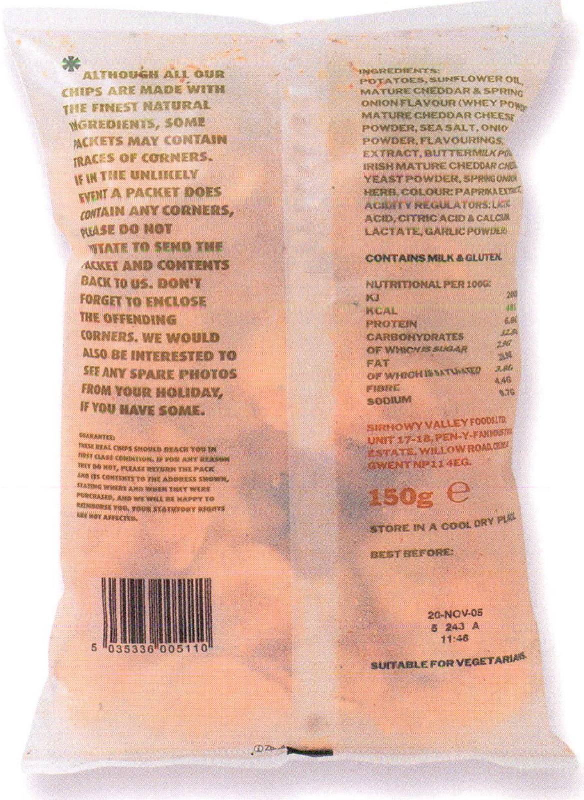

REAL.
EVER TRIED TO BLEND
MATURE CHEDDAR
& SPRING ONION
FLAVOURS TOGETHER? WELL IT'S NOT
EASY. SOMETIMES WE CAN HARDLY
SEE WHAT WE'RE DOING FOR
WEEPING. AND THE MATURITY OF
THE CHEDDAR MAKES US FEEL ALL
SILLY AND CHILDISH IN COMPARISON.
WE PREVAIL AS THESE HANDCOOKED
CHIPS ARE OUR LABOUR OF LOVE AND
BECAUSE IT'S IN OUR NATURE NOT TO
CUT CORNERS.
150g ℮

ALTHOUGH ALL OUR
CHIPS ARE MADE WITH
THE FINEST NATURAL
TRACES OF CORNERS.
BACK TO US. DON'T
FORGET TO ENCLOSE
THE OFFENDING
CORNERS. WE WOULD
ALSO BE INTERESTED TO
SEE ANY SPARE PHOTOS
FROM YOUR HOLIDAY,
IF YOU HAVE SOME.
CONTAINS MILK & GLUTEN.
150g ℮
BEST BEFORE:
20-NOV-05
5 243 A
11:46
5 035336 005110

opportunity for them to respond (beyond making a purchase, if it was that sort of job). The arrival of social media means this monologue has been at least partly replaced by dialogue, as individuals and brands exchange thoughts on everything from new business ideas to corporate social responsibility. As a result, copywriters working for these brands need to know how to open and sustain a conversation in writing[2].

...It all comes back to brands

Almost all copywriters, regardless of their particular employer or industry niche, are concerned with brands. They might express this concern in different ways, but underneath the sector-specific jargon is a near-universal

2. It also means readers are far less passive than in the past. In fact you could say readers aren't really readers any more; in the digital world they're often active contributors to the debate—"the people formerly known as 'the audience'"—as US cultural critic Clay Shirky describes them in his book, *Cognitive Surplus*.

Chapter Three

THE THREE Ellipsis sisters insisted on doing everything together. They wore the same clothes, ate the same food and listened to the same music. Their parents christened them Dorothy, Doritella and Dottina but most often people referred to them as Dot, Dot, Dot.

At school, they were exceptionally well-rounded, careful to dot every single i. (Though friendly with the T's, they studiously avoided crossing them.)

Nonetheless, many of their classmates found them aloof. Perhaps it was because they had a bad habit of leaving conversations hanging…

Or maybe it was because sometimes they would suddenly pause…

…for an excruciatingly long time.

One evening after a poetry class, Dot, Dot and Dot found themselves surrounded by several angry Words. Fed up with having their sentences rudely interrupted, they decided to teach the girls a lesson.

Fortunately, some Commas intervened and managed to separate them.

After several tense moments, the entire commotion came to a full stop. Nobody was injured but the sisters vowed that wasn't the end of the matter…

38   There's life in a book

never suspected the attention paid to him. He repeatedly mumbled, "Thank you! Thank you! Thank you!" as he backed awkwardly out of the room.

22. SIGNS OF LOVE

FROM THE DAY HE WAS BORN, Exclamation Mark had very strong opinions. Worse still, he always insisted on sharing them in an extremely loud voice. His mother tolerated his assertive behaviour until she almost went deaf. Finally, she kicked him out of the house.

And that's when he met her, the alluring and very mysterious Question Mark. She had a beautiful face, a slender line and curves in all the right places. She was curious about everything.

Exclamation Mark was instantly attracted to her and took great pride in explaining what he knew. What he didn't know, he simply over-emphasised. They enjoyed each other's company and were often seen queuing together at the end of the line.

One thing led to another and they soon decided to marry. However, the state flatly objected on the grounds of incest. Apparently, they came from the same family.

With nowhere to go, they decided to elope. To avoid attracting attention, Exclamation Mark changed his name to Exclamation Point whilst Question Mark disguised herself as a Spaniard by standing on her head.

These days, they can be found spending their evenings alone, punctuating the awkward silence.

There's life in a book

Wordy ads for word lovers. How appropriate for a publisher like Penguin.

---

interest in helping their client's brand grow and prosper. That's why we've included a lesson on the B word later in this book—building and sustaining brands is the engine behind much of what we do, so it pays to have a solid understanding of how brands work. For now just be aware that, in the end, 99 percent of copywriting is somehow in the service of brands.[3]

…Persuasion and engagement

In her book *The Idea Writers*, Teressa Iezzi argues:

> Now the copywriter's job is to create stuff that people love and engage with and respond to and even become disciples of. That's what's changed— and it's a good thing […] advertising was all about persuasion. Now it's all about engagement.

That may be true for advertising copywriters, but is it true for their branding brethren? Surely we need a bit

3. Possible exceptions include public information campaigns, government work, and certain types of charity writing. In these situations communicating information tends to take precedence over brand building.

Chris Waite

"Nobody reads ads."

As the quotation marks indicate, I didn't write that headline.

Step forward Mr. Howard Luck Gossage, variously described as "the Socrates of San Francisco," "America's most influential advertising genius," and "the Velvet Underground to Ogilvy's Beatles."

Encouragingly, what Gossage went on to say was "People read what interests them. Sometimes, it's an ad." Phew—so the copywriter's efforts are not in vain after all...sometimes.

Copywriting differs from most other forms of professional writing—journalism, for example—in that, sadly, the only people likely to be on the edge of their seats, agog with anticipation at the prospect of your latest pronouncement, are your mom and the client. If journalism is ephemeral, copywriting must be little more than antimatter.

My first piece of advice, then, is to remember the default position: Right now, no one out there is the slightest bit bothered about your client's product or your ad.

Second, this leads to a pretty obvious sequitur: Keep it interesting. Is what you've written motivating? Would it really interest people? *Really?* Read your copy out loud and see how it sounds. Be honest with yourself; and if that doesn't work, ask your spouse, partner, housemate, and/or drinking buddy for their opinion.

Third, get to know not just the product, but also your target audience. They may be very different from you—in age, sex, politics, religion, assumptions, priorities. Never assume everyone thinks the same way you do.

Fourth: The brief is your friend (assuming it's a decent brief). Refer back to it constantly. It's all too easy to get blocked in a creative cul-de-sac unless you take the time to think your argument through first.

That brings us to our fifth point. Clarity before cleverness. Whether you're striving for the perfect headline, tagline, piece of dialogue, or caption, if you can't think of a form of words you feel is brilliant enough, don't sit there fuming. Just start writing. Even if you will never use long copy in your campaign, write an essay about the product. Concentrate on being clear and persuasive rather than clever. If you're a real writer, you will find the cleverness starts to creep in without you even noticing.

Next: In the search for clear, effective communication, be prepared to chuck out redundant phrases, sentences, even whole paragraphs you have carved to perfection and now love. It's a cruel old world.

My final point is, give the writing a rest every so often. Just save what you've written and go for a walk, see a movie, visit your local purveyor of Flat White. Think about something else for a while, then come back to it. Read what you've written. And then—with a bit of luck—you won't be the only person who does.

Chris is senior lecturer and course leader on the highly regarded Creative Advertising MA course at University College Falmouth in the UK. He arrived there after 30 years as a copywriter and then creative director for a succession of top London advertising agencies (including Saatchi & Saatchi, Leagas Delaney, Publicis, and Grey) where he cocreated award-winning campaigns for clients ranging from breweries to building societies. Chris's research interests in recent years have concentrated heavily on the effects of the digital media revolution on the advertising business.

A great campaign for cheap and cheerful electrical retailer Dixons' online offer, which plays on the universal desire for a bargain.

Get off at the fashionable end of Oxford Street, drift into the achingly cool technology hall of London's most happening department store and view this year's must-have plasma courtesy of the sound and vision technologist in the Marc Jacobs sandals then go to dixons.co.uk and buy it.

Dixons.co.uk
The last place you want to go

Get off at Knightsbridge, visit the discerning shopper's fave department store, ascend the exotic staircase and let Piers in the pinstripe suit demonstrate the magic of the latest high-definition flatscreen then go to dixons.co.uk and buy it.

Dixons.co.uk
The last place you want to go

of both—persuasion without engagement is cold and grudging; engagement without persuasion is fruitless and ultimately unrewarding. The first step in persuading someone is to engage them. So a recurring theme in this book is "Don't be boring" a phrase borrowed from David Abbott, one of the UK's best ever advertising copywriters.

...Learn from everything, steal from anywhere
We're not saying lift the work of others wholesale—that's called plagiarism and it's wrong in a very real legal sense; we're saying grab what inspires you and make it your own. Because in the end we can't really do anything else—our consciousness is a product of our experience, a kaleidoscope of everything we've ever

been exposed to. The trick is to absorb what appeals, then twist it to suit your purposes (actually that's two tricks but you get the point). In the end you're only as good as the stuff you surround yourself with, so seek out the widest possible range of inputs, soak up the genius of others like a quilted paper towel, and don't worry too much about originality. Nothing comes out of nothing; there's a precursor to everything, and when people say "How original!", what they really mean is they don't recognize its sources.

...Persistence pays

If working with words was easy, lots of people would be doing it. But it's not, it's hard—hard to land your first job (and your second, and your third...), hard to learn everything you need to succeed (although this book is here to help), and hard to stay fresh (without which you'll turn into a drudge). However you look at it, building a career as a copywriter requires an industrial-sized dose of persistence. Here's Benjamin Franklin, one of the Founding Fathers, on the merits of terrier-like tenacity:

> Energy and persistence conquer all things.

Over a century later another politician—Calvin Coolidge—made much the same point:

> Press on. Nothing in the world can take the place of Persistence. Talent will not; nothing is more common than unsuccessful men with talent. Genius will not; unrewarded genius is almost a proverb. Education will not; the world is full of educated derelicts. Persistence and determination alone are omnipotent. The slogan "Press On" has solved and always will solve the problems of the human race.

And on that empowering note let's take Coolidge's advice and, well, press on.

Now you have a go

Perhaps it's a bit early to ask you to put what you've learned into practice, but if you're up for it, here are a couple of exercises to try. Do give them a go—copywriting is something you learn by doing, and you want your money's worth from this book, don't you?

As with all the workouts included in the book, when you've finished, ask yourself, "What stood out as I was working through? What have I learned? How can I apply it to my own writing?" Make notes, and refer to them often. That way you'll really get the benefit.

Workout One

Brand copywriters need to be confident working with texts that are measured in paragraphs and pages rather than syllables and sentences, so to sharpen your skills we want you to write us a long-copy piece on "Why everyone should commit an imprisonable offense some time in their lives." Call it an article, a rant, an essay, an ad, a propaganda piece—we don't mind. All that matters is that you make your writing so fabulously irresistible that the reader can't help wishing it were longer. That's your goal—leave 'em wanting more.[4] Somewhere between 100 and 300 words should do it.

Workout Two

Same again, only this time write us a compelling piece on "The case for cheating on your partner."

4. Often described as "The first rule of showbiz."

Lesson Two:
The Right Way to Write

Doing the basics brilliantly

This pre-Christmas copy gets straight to the point.

Here we explain the key principles of effective copywriting; in the next we introduce you to a series of techniques to make your work all but irresistible. Think of Lessons Two and Three as a crash course in the principles and practice of great copywriting.

Consider, if you will, the following response from E. B. White, author of *Charlotte's Web* and *Stuart Little,* to a fan inquiring about his admirably stripped-down prose style:

There are very few thoughts or concepts that can't be put into plain English, provided anyone truly wants to do it. But for everyone who strives for clarity and simplicity, there are three who for one reason or another prefer to draw the clouds across the sky.

As well as being a highly successful writer of children's fiction, White was also co-author of *The Elements of Style*, one of the most important books on composition and form ever published.[1] Written by William Strunk in 1918 and significantly revised by White in 1959, *Strunk and White* (as it's usually called) has helped generations of authors improve their prose.

We mention this because (a) you could do a lot worse than acquire a copy of this pithy little book as bedtime reading and (b) White's point that pretty much anything can be explained with clarity and simplicity is at the heart of this lesson. The process we describe in the following pages is ideal for any situation where you need to get your message across in strong, straightforward terms. We suggest you internalize it and make it your default approach—it'll help you create effective base texts you can then build on to produce something more ambitious.

Remember, your work doesn't have to be brilliant straight away—in fact it almost certainly won't be. Getting a decent first draft down is a great confidence boost and the best—perhaps only—way to produce a second version with more magic. As Luke Sullivan, author of *Hey Whipple, Squeeze This: The Classic Guide to Creating Great Ads* and a contributor to this book, puts it, "First write it straight, then write it great." Lesson Two is about straight, Lesson Three is about great.

One last point before we proceed. We've called this lesson "The right way to write" but of course there's no "right way." If our advice genuinely feels wrong then it probably is—at least for you. If it comes to a contest between your instincts and this book then go with your guts every time.

1. *Elements* has also come in for plenty of criticism, with detractors labelling it po-faced and appealing only to pedants. You decide.

This napkin is 100% recyclable (Pret's sustainability department is militant, we're making headway). If Pret staff get all serviette-ish and hand you huge bunches of napkins (which you don't need or want) please give them the evil eye. Waste not want not.

The humble napkin, transformed into a billboard for the brand's environmental ambitions. They deserve a medal for "serviette-ish" alone.

Four steps to copy heaven

No one sits down at a computer or with a notebook and magically creates clear, compelling copy. It might *look* like that's what they're doing, but that's only because they've internalized the approach we're about to describe. No, going from nothing to something is a four-stage process during which you **research**, **plan**, **write**, and **review**.

Amid all the brouhaha about carbon emissions, this straightforward message from Italian furniture-design company Lago feels like a breath of fresh air.

Step 1—Research

Scrimp on research and you'll be struggling to make up for it throughout the writing process. It's not just about gathering facts and figures—essential though that is—it's about finding a way into your raw material and establishing the "personal truth" of your subject (to borrow a phrase from Dan Wieden, founder of über ad agency Wieden+Kennedy).

Research starts with reading the brief. In fact don't read it—interrogate it mercilessly until it reveals its secrets. They are the foundations on which the rest of your work should build.

The brief is of course the document that defines the project and your part in it. We say "document" but neatly typed letter-size sheets are the exception; more likely, your so-called brief will be buried in the body of an e-mail or form part of a hurried conversation in less than ideal conditions. The important thing to remember is this: Regardless of how your brief arrives, you need to dig deep until you're 100 percent clear about

- The nature of the job
- The identity of the audience
- The problem you're trying to solve
- The big idea you need to build on
- Any key messages your copy must contain
- The tone or personality of the finished piece
- When it needs to be done by
- Where to go for further information

What are you waiting for?

A change? Something new and different? A challenge, perhaps? Or maybe you never wait for anything.

After all, people with drive don't wait, do they? They go out and get. Waiting is passive. Boring. A waste of time.

But wait. Is that always the case? Granted, hanging around for a bus is dull. Waiting for someone or something that could change your life, the lives of others and even the safety and security of a whole country is, well, a lot more interesting.

You've read this far. You're in a minority. Only 17% of people ever read adverts past the headline. Assuming, of course, this is an advert. There's no logo, no obvious contact details and no product. You'll have to read on to find out more. Wait a little longer.

Of course, you could skip to the end, but will you get the full story? You see we're looking for people who can handle detail. Men and women with patience and determination. You see, we don't care what sex you are or where you're from. We don't even care what you do now, only what you can do.

That said, you probably already have a successful career in academia or the public sector. Or perhaps you're thriving in the high-octane world of finance or commerce. Your peers see you as dynamic. Your bosses may have you ear-marked for promotion. But there's something missing: A nagging feeling that you could be doing something more worthwhile. Something more rewarding, but not simply in a financial way.

Well, that paragraph will have lost us a few more readers. But you're still with us. Good. Hopefully that means you're the contradictory sort of person we might be interested in: Dynamic, but patient. A team player that can work with complete autonomy. Someone who can form strong relationships, yet thrive in the isolation of a foreign country. Who is already in successful employment with a credible history of commercial success, but who wants a change. A British national with the cultural sensitivity to seamlessly integrate into the day-to-day society of a different country. Someone with a consuming political curiosity, who believes in the importance of promoting and protecting British interests, both at home and abroad.

By reading between the lines, you've probably guessed what we're after. But we're not interested in people who trust to guesswork. As we said before, patience is rewarded and so you'll find out more about MI6 at sis.gov.uk/careers. We're nearly at the end, so to get this far you're hopefully interested in what you've read. You may even be considering applying. You may feel like talking to friends or family about this. That's completely natural and will end your application process before it's even started. So if you want to discuss applying, discuss it with us and no one else.

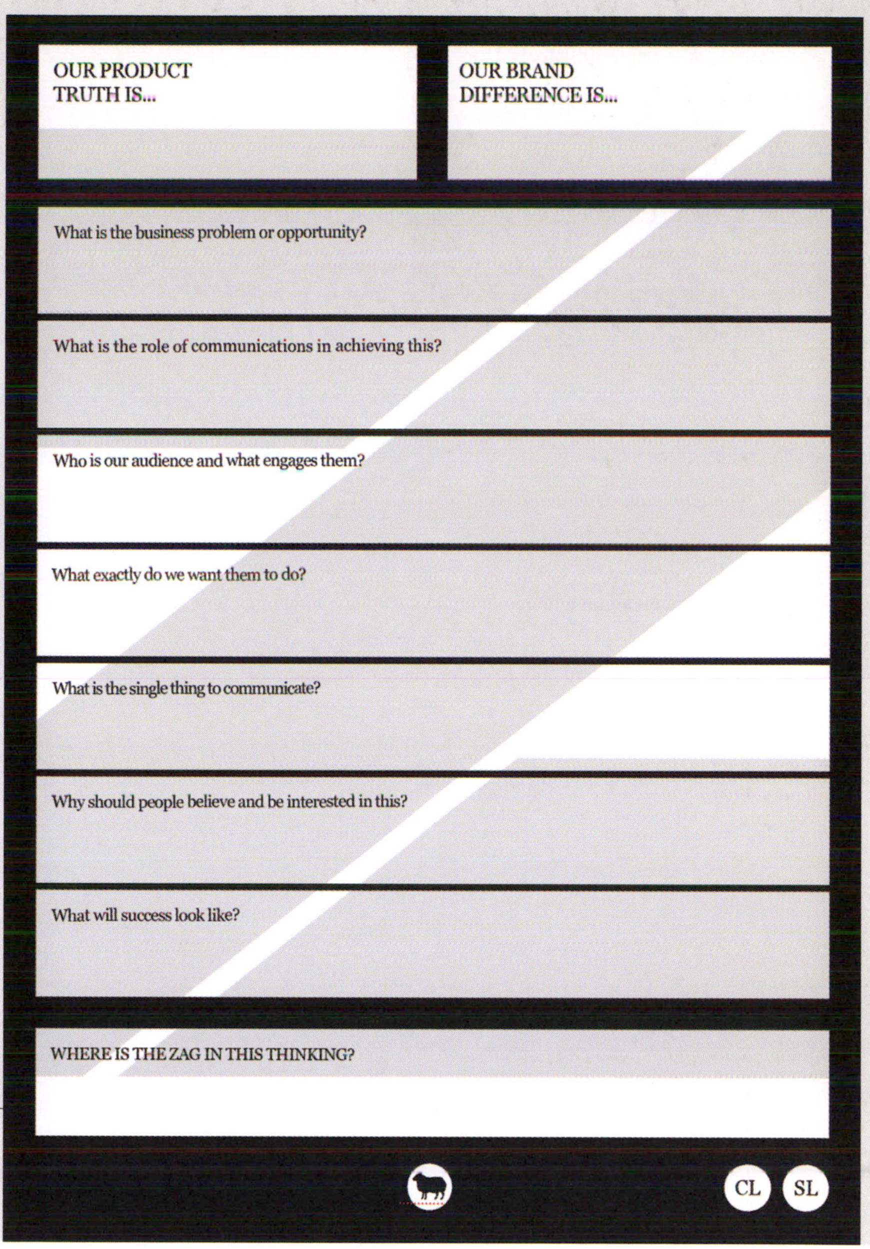

OUR PRODUCT TRUTH IS...

OUR BRAND DIFFERENCE IS...

What is the business problem or opportunity?

What is the role of communications in achieving this?

Who is our audience and what engages them?

What exactly do we want them to do?

What is the single thing to communicate?

Why should people believe and be interested in this?

What will success look like?

WHERE IS THE ZAG IN THIS THINKING?

CL   SL

Intelligent stuff from M&C Saatchi for Britain's MI6 intelligence agency. Notice how the text messes with your mind, taking you down one train of thought before suddenly switching to another—like the job it advertises.

A brief template from BBH. A well-written and well-organized brief should contain all the information you need to get started.

There are 101 other things you might need to know, but these are the absolute essentials.

And what do you do if you don't receive anything resembling a brief as described above? Why, you write your own. We don't mean you make it up (at least you don't *admit* to making it up); instead you unearth the information listed above for yourself. Never blame others for the scantiness of a brief (even if it's their fault)—make it your business to uncover everything you need to succeed. If you don't and the resulting

work is off-target, no one will blame your briefer; they'll blame you. Tiresome though it sounds, you really *do* need to know what you're supposed to be doing before you start doing it.

One of the most important things the brief should tell you is who you're writing for. We've dedicated a whole lesson to this later in the book, but for now we'll just say you must know who your readers are in order to write effectively for them. "Must" is a strong word, but it's the right one in this context. Your reader's hopes,

Chain stitching.
It means you could cut the
stitching with a knife
and it still wouldn't unravel.
Alternatively you could
buy ordinary jeans and not
cut the stitching with a knife.

howies.co.uk

above: This eccentric fact about chain
stitching could only come from digging deep.

opposite: It would be hard—maybe even
impossible—to write copy like this if
you'd never spent a night under canvas.

dreams, anxieties, prejudices, problems, and so on
should form a sort of filter through which you sift the
raw material you collect during this phase, enabling
you to make it relevant. And none of that can happen if
you don't know who you're supposed to be talking to.

Finally, it's impossible to write well about something
you don't understand, so the Research stage is about
saturating yourself in the subject. Make notes. Draw
diagrams. Talk to people—lots of people. Ask questions
—lots of questions. Build up a library of information to
power your prose once you start writing. Make your
desk groan under the weight of your research. As long
as you keep it relevant, there's no such thing as too
much background material.

Well, *almost* no such thing. If you're particularly lucky/
zealous then you may face the problem of information
overload, especially if time is tight and you're not
permitted the luxury of assimilation. The solution is
knowing what you can safely ignore. That calls for
confidence, and *that* comes from knowing exactly what
you're trying to do—which comes back to the brief. The
better your understanding of your task,
the better you'll be able to judge what's ignorable.

THE MILLETS DELUXE FAMILY TENT PACK. £149.99

INCLUDES

1 three-room, four-person tent
4 sleeping bags
2 roll mats
1 double airbed
8 gobsmackingly beautiful sunsets
5 blackbird wake-up calls
2 glorious days without a phone signal
1 cowpat incident
3 scary campfire stories
1 rather dull campfire story
4 pees behind trees
1 grasshopper solo
16 hot chocolates
1 brother-on-sister assault *(dead leg)*
5 games of 'I spy'
1 sister-on-brother assault *(Chinese burn)*
3 rude awakenings by some very loud snores
1 bizarrely smelly hedgerow
2 messy grass stains on your knees
1 attempt to wash clothes in a river
5 butterfly chases
1 'plastic plate versus paper plate' debate
15 dandelions
1 trillion dandelion seeds
3 atishoos
2 occasions when you trip over the guy ropes
1 zap by an electric fence
3 marshmallows stuck on a stick
5 failed attempts to identify Orion's Belt
1 huge moan about not having a hairdryer
7 eerie noises in the middle of the night
6 splashes in puddles
4 sploshes
2 splishes
20 minutes making daisy chains
40 matches that won't light
1 dawning realisation the matchbox is wet
1 cry of 'Ouch! Blasted thistle!'
8 sheep that won't be stroked
2 hours spent making clouds look like faces
14 campfire sing-alongs
1 campfire sing-along *(in tune)*
10 muddy fingernails
2 minutes spent reading a map upside down

3 shouts of 'Are we there yet?'
4 games of Pooh-sticks
5 burnt sausages *(inedible)*
1 burnt sausage *(sort of edible)*
1 knot-tying session
2 tree-climbing sessions
3 rolling-down-the-hill sessions
30 seconds of feeling really dizzy
1 pair of pants lost in your sleeping bag
1 river crossing
2 waterlogged wellies
1 fruitless search for kindling
1 plastic plate melting on the barbecue
1 intimate moment *(interrupted)*
3 chats with a friendly farmer
6 long country walks
1 morning spent nursing blisters
1 large, unidentified creepy-crawly
3 ladybirds
8 picnics
1 stubbed toe
1 peat bog *(really boggy)*
5 shooting stars
½ an earthworm
6 games of football *(boys only)*
1 snail in the shower
8 lazy afternoons
2 games of rounders *(girls only)*
15 nasty nettle stings
1 search for dock leaves
3 hissy fits
1 scream of 'Where's the loo roll?'
1 dead rabbit discovery
3 hills you run down very fast
15 skims of a stone *(personal best)*
1 hole accidentally burnt in your fleece
1 mole trying to burrow under the tent
1 stumble over a stupid rock
9 beautiful dewy mornings
25,063 cubic metres of fresh air

Gyles and Roger's mind map for Lesson Six of this very book. It ain't pretty, but neither are they.

Step 2—Plan

The Planning stage is where you clarify the problem your readers are facing and the solution your product/service/brand is offering. In some cases this will be straightforward ("Embarrassing personal itching? You need our new super-strength antifungal cream!"). But in other situations the problem is less clear-cut. If you're writing a marketing campaign for an art gallery there's no "problem" as such. However, there might be a need, in this case, for a bit more culture in one's life. So take a broad view of "problem" and "solution" but get to the bottom of them just the same.

Among other things, the Planning stage is where you get the thinking right.

Of course when your client/boss is screaming for it yesterday then the luxury of creative reflection is the first thing to go, along with lunch, going home at a reasonable hour, and other such nonessentials. Except that getting the thinking right is far from nonessential—in fact nothing is more important.

The best approach we've found is to have a conversation with yourself. Find a quietish place or go for a walk and just ask yourself what you're *really* trying to do here. If you're stuck use the classic who/what/where/when/why/how list. Aim to get it down to a phrase or sentence. As always with planning, the more effort you put in here, the faster you'll progress once you start the actual writing.

Once you're truly clear about your challenge you can use this insight to whip the raw material you gathered during the Research phase into shape. Perhaps the easiest way to begin is by creating a "mind map," with the key phrase or sentence that emerged during your internal conversation at its center. Getting your main themes down on paper like this will show where your train of thought is strongest and where it needs more work. It might also reveal connections between secondary ideas you hadn't previously considered.

If you've several points to cover you'll need to find some sort of connection or flow. In practice this means looking at your mind map and exploring different sequences of your main themes. Try a few alternative orders to see which works best, all the while remembering why your reader is reading your piece in the first place, and what they want out of it. Exactly how you structure your piece will depend on your audience, your subject, and your goal, although the following tried-and-true approaches should get you started.

Issues>implications>actions
Ideal for short documents. You tee up the issues, explain their implications, and suggest some appropriate action.

Past>present>future
Explain how something came to be, what the current situation looks like, and where it could go next.

Context>analysis>conclusion>actions
This slightly more detailed structure works well for longer pieces. An alternative version that's particularly useful for anything reportlike is *Issue>background>current situation> conclusion>suggestions*.

Problem>solution>results
The classic case-study format. Not particularly imaginative in its naked form but a solid basis on which to build.

Inverted triangle
The classic newspaper-story format. Start with a grabby headline, followed by the main points, before moving to detailed information and analysis.

Goal>step one>step two>step X>result
The classic instruction format. Start by describing what this process will achieve, then take your readers through the process step by step (beginning each step with a verb, because that's the correct way to present any instruction). End by describing where they should be now.

Q&A
If you're aware of the questions a reader might ask then cut to the chase and just answer them. Obviously this depends on knowing what your audience are actually after—there's nothing quite as sad as Frequently Asked Questions that no one asks, frequently or otherwise. They make a brand look lazy and irrelevant.

Big Bang

Sun Forms

Planets Orbit

Earth Cools

Rock Crushes

Diamonds Form

Amoeba

Dinosaurs

Man

Man Digs Up
Diamonds

Rosendorff Man
Buys Diamonds

Man Gives
Diamond To Woman

Big Bang

ROSENDORFF

Andi Teran

Ask any wordsmith about their criteria for writing and the chances are you'll get a one-word answer: storytelling. They'll often follow this up with how difficult it is to get the story just right. It can be a battle, and the way to win is through a combination of observation, imagination, and tenacity.

As a journalist and blogger I rely on observation before beginning the writing process. This is my favorite part because it feels as if I'm not doing very much even though I'm building the foundation of my entire piece.

Observation gets you in the "write" frame of mind—forgive the pun, but it's true. I've covered New York Fashion Week for several years. If you think that means watching models walk by in various ensembles you're absolutely correct. But it's much more than that. Before I walk into the auditorium I'm already taking notes. What do people look like and what are they discussing? What's the ambience? Is anything amiss? What's the overall energy of the place? It's much more than just jotting down clothing notes.

All these observations help the writing process, even if I never use the actual information I've collected. They help me answer my own questions and often catalyze a more in-depth or descriptive view of whatever it is I'm writing about.

Listening is also a key component. My work sometimes sees me interviewing actors, directors, and musicians, and listening is half the job. If you can't give your subject your full attention, you'll miss the good stuff. And if you aren't prepared, you'll have a difficult time focusing on your client or subject.

I once interviewed a somewhat shy musician, and I struggled to get them to open up and reveal something interesting about themselves and the album they were promoting. Then I remembered a book we'd both read. I mentioned this and the mood changed. We both relaxed and an interesting conversation began. When it came time to write my piece, I had so much more to work with.

You have to be willing to give more than you might get. You have to put in the work. And you need to give yourself a break and have fun with it when you get stuck. Writing is a self-reliant process.

Andi is a writer and performer living in Los Angeles. Her words have appeared in *Vanity Fair, Monocle, Bloomberg Businessweek*, and the *Paris Review*. She has written and performed for stages throughout the US, and her haiku poetry was featured on CBS *Sunday Morning*. In between taco tastings and cacti cultivation, she volunteers for the Young Storytellers Foundation and rants on her blog verbosecoma.com. She is currently at work on her first novel.

If that's not a product benefit we don't know what is.

Step 3—Write

If we had to summarize *Read Me* in one sentence it would be this: Write like you speak, but speak well. This isn't a particularly original idea—many people have said much the same thing over the years. The great adman David Ogilvy remarked, "I spend my life speaking well of products in advertisements." Henry Ford advised his dealers to "solicit by personal visitation." Clearly that's not practical for most organizations, so copy that does the same job is the next best thing.[2]

As we suggested in the last lesson, effective copy tends to adopt the rhythms of speech. The tone of this exchange can be anywhere from thoroughly formal through to ridiculously relaxed, depending on the brand, the occasion, the medium and a host of other factors, but where possible we suggest you aim for a conversational feel. The great novelist Elmore Leonard summed this up nicely when he said,

"If it sounds like writing, I rewrite it."

But how exactly *do* you write in a way that doesn't sound like writing? As we've already suggested, start by deciding what you'd say if you were speaking to your reader, then simply write it down.[3] Another useful

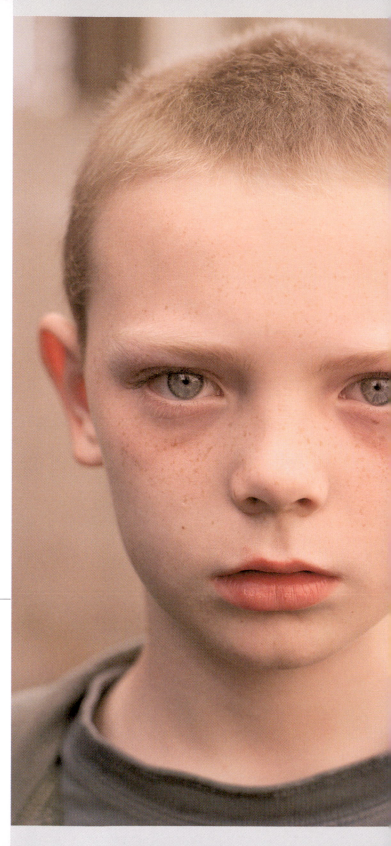

The power of "we." It says, "Here's a peek into our world; maybe you like what you see."

2. The following quote provides a peek into Ogilvy's world: "When you sit down to write your copy, pretend you are talking to the woman on your right at a dinner party. She has asked you, 'I am thinking of buying a new car. Which would you recommend?' Write as if you are answering that question." Patronizing as can be, but Ogilvy's advice is sound—write like you speak, just speak well.

3. In our writing workshops people often ask us for advice on how to express a particular point, usually beginning their query with the words, "I want to say…." To which we reply, "If that's what you want to say then just go ahead and say it." It's great to see the lightbulb come on over their heads as they realize they already know the answer.

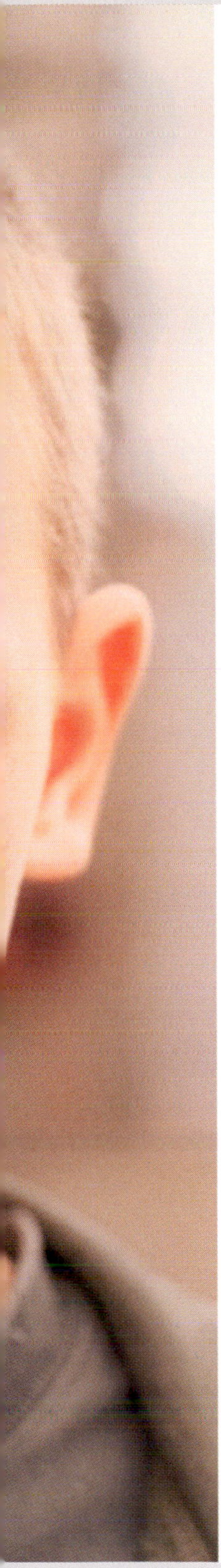

He told his parents to fk off. He told his foster parents to f**k off. He told fourteen social workers to f**k off. He told us to f**k off. But we didn't. And we still haven't.**

There are thousands of disadvantaged children in the UK. Many of them have stories that would break your heart. Some of them are capable of terrible things. But if, like us, you believe that no child is born bad, then you can't watch someone get dumped into the file marked 'problem'. You can't let society play pass the parcel with a young person's life. If a child is referred to Barnardo's we stick by that child. We listen. We look for potential. We give practical support. And if we don't give up on the troubled, young boy, it's not because we enjoy being sworn at, it's because we believe in him.

To show you believe in children, text 'Believe' to 84862 or visit barnardos.org.uk

Believe in children

🌳 Barnardo's

The power of "you." It's strangely
magnetic; we can't help but look.

approach is to pay attention to pronouns. Use the
first person (*I*, *we*, *us*, *our*) for warmth and to express
subjective opinions. Use the third (*s/he*, *it*, *they*, *its*,
their) for formality and to make objective points—the
third person literally distances the writer and reader
from the subject, positioning them as observers and
not participants in the conversation. Use a combination
of first person and second person (*you*, *your*) to create
a direct relationship and establish a dialogue between
writer and reader.

Not every organization will go along with the first-
person familiarity we've just recommended, but if you're
speaking on behalf of a business it makes sense to use
"we" instead of "the board" or whatever. Using personal
pronouns enables you to build a closer connection
between brand and reader with all the benefits that
brings. Where possible, it pays to get personal.

Let's move on. It's important to understand that the
writing stage is often a process of translation where
you take raw research and convert it into polished
prose that fulfills a particular purpose. You need to get
good at this; the chances are, some variation of this
translation process will form a large part of your
professional life. Lord Rutherford, the father of
nuclear physics, advised his underlings:

"If you can't explain your physics to a barmaid, it is bad physics."

Despite the implied slur on barmaids his Lordship was
spot on—clear explanations come from clear thinking
and real understanding. What we're saying is, be aware
of your place in the communications process—it's *you*
who sits between your subject and your audience, and
it's you who makes the former palatable to the latter.

How do you do this? Remember your readers. As we
explain in Lesson Five, the simple way to do this is to ask
yourself what you'd want to see if you were in their shoes.
Let this simple insight steer your whole translation.

At the same time, it's important to pay attention to the
form of your words. When we speak we unconsciously
vary the length of our sentences; when we write we
should aim to do the same. The simple way to check
this is to read your words aloud (or at least under your

Google's literal take on "write like you speak."

breath). Not only will this highlight any awkward phrases or dodgy syntax, it'll also show where your flow ain't flowing and your meaning ain't meaningful. Reading back what you've written should become as natural as hitting the Save icon.

It also pays to keep your paragraphs tight—in most situations five sentences are plenty. If a paragraph is running away with you then divide it in two. In fact, try to keep your whole piece as short as possible. We doubt anyone ever finished a piece of copy and wistfully sighed, "I just wish it were longer."

Finally, a really useful technique for the Writing stage is to create a "core story." This is just a fancy phrase for a document that contains everything important about your subject, written up under appropriate headings to a good (but not finished) standard. It's a content pool

that will itself never see the light of day—it's almost certainly too long, for a start—but it can be a really useful resource during the Writing stage and is a great technique for ongoing projects that need multiple expressions of the same basic material.

Here's how it works. Imagine you've been given the job of writing marketing material for a technology trade show. It's an open-ended, ongoing job so you decide to put in a couple of late nights creating a detailed core story that will act as your copy repository. The result is perhaps three sides of paper, covering everything significant about said show. Imagine your satisfaction when the following day you're asked to put together an HTML e-mail promoting the show's launch—by lunchtime. Because you've already gathered everything you need in the form of your core story it's incredibly

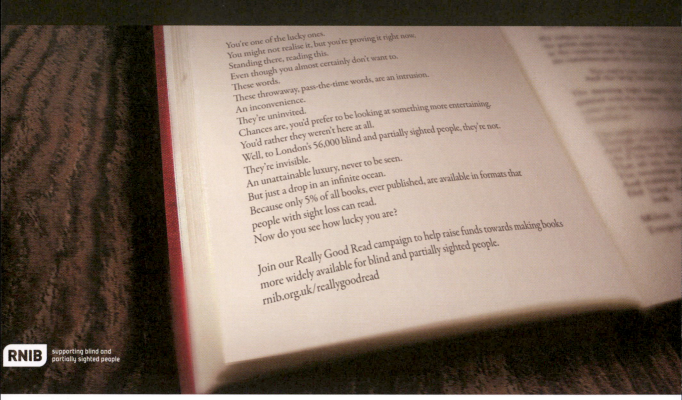

You're one of the lucky ones.
You might not realise it, but you're proving it right now.
Standing there, reading this.
Even though you almost certainly don't want to.
These words.
These throwaway, pass-the-time words, are an intrusion.
An inconvenience.
They're uninvited.
Chances are, you'd prefer to be looking at something more entertaining.
You'd rather they weren't here at all.
Well, to London's 56,000 blind and partially sighted people, they're not.
They're invisible.
An unattainable luxury, never to be seen.
But just a drop in an infinite ocean.
Because only 5% of all books, ever published, are available in formats that
people with sight loss can read.
Now do you see how lucky you are?

Join our Really Good Read campaign to help raise funds towards making books
more widely available for blind and partially sighted people.
rnib.org.uk/reallygoodread

RNIB supporting blind and partially sighted people

easy for you to grab a sentence from here and a paragraph from there to quickly assemble 99 percent finished copy. A quick polish and you're done.

Then, two days later, you're asked to put together a leaflet and some big banners to go in the show's entrance hall; again you dip into your core story, pick the bits you need, and away you go. The following morning they're screaming for a microsite, and again you dip and build in record time, earning the admiration of all who know you. So yes, creating a core story means a little extra work upfront, but it also means less work later as you'll already have everything you need. In the right situation it's a great technique and one we thoroughly recommend.

Taking a soft approach can deliver hard results. Here the friendly tone helps establish a rapport that makes a donation far more likely.

Step 4—Review

This is where you read over what you've done to make sure it does what it's supposed to do. Reviewing is the polishing process during which you turn your sow's ear of a first draft into the silk purse of your finished piece. That won't happen in one pass—chances are you'll need to go over your copy again and again, smoothing out imperfections and correcting shortcomings by degrees until you're thoroughly sick of the wretched thing. Just remember: Every tiny tweak brings it closer to God.

It's during the Review stage that you check you've done what the brief asked you to do. As your teachers no doubt told you at exam time, "Don't write what you want to write, *write what the question asks for.*" It's exactly the same with copywriting; don't hand in some impressive but irrelevant wordplay; instead, make sure you know exactly what you're trying to do—and when you're finished, make sure you've done it. To do that we suggest you reread the brief. Even if you're certain you've understood it, it's worth checking your work against the brief one more time to make sure you haven't inadvertently strayed into irrelevancy.

Perhaps our choicest piece of guidance for this stage is, "If in doubt, cut it out." It isn't always clear if a word, sentence, or paragraph should make the final version. If you can't decide whether to hit the Delete key or not, here's our advice—do it. If you're asking yourself "Should I/shouldn't I?" then you've already highlighted a problem and you need to fix it. It might seem harsh, but we suggest you don't give borderline cases the benefit of the doubt. If that really troubles you then

THE DAVID CORNFIELD
MELANOMA FUND
WAS ESTABLISHED IN MEMORY OF DAVID CORNFIELD
TO FULFIL HIS GOAL OF REDUCING THE NUMBER OF SKIN CANCER CASES
BY RAISING AWARENESS OF THE DISEASE.
PLEASE EXPLORE OUR SITE TO FIND OUT MORE ABOUT OUR PLANS AND HOW YOU CAN CONTRIBUTE.

A series of people who've beaten skin cancer offer advice to their younger selves, ranging from the cheery ("Dear 16-year-old me, please don't get that perm, it's not as awesome as you think") to the serious ("This is a cancer that shows on the outside. Start checking your skin now"). The result is funny, smart, moving, and generally wonderful. See the whole thing at www.dcmf.ca.

Nick Law

If you can think clearly, and tell people what you're thinking without boring them, you can probably write. Although this seems simple, two things tend to get in the way of good copywriting: bad craft and overused words.

In a sense grammarians are right; craft comes from learning the rules that govern a written language. But craft mostly comes from writing a lot. The best writers have a confidence and mastery born of endless hours at the keyboard. If you want to be a good writer you need to write everyday.

The more a metaphor, simile, or other figure of speech is used in popular media, the easier it is to ignore. Don't get into the habit of using overused words. Just parroting what you've heard before is lazy. This is a particular problem in marketing, a world that seems to make a virtue of using pretentious compound words when everyday English would be far better. Nothing masks meaning more effectively than jargon.

Writing well is not easy, but getting better is not complicated. Simply write a lot and write simply.

....

Nick is Global Chief Creative Officer at R/GA, one of the most respected digital ad agencies in the world. He began his career in design/corporate identity (including stints at FutureBrand in New York and Pentagram in London under the guidance of the legendary Alan Fletcher and John McConnell) before moving into advertising, and now works on both the traditional and interactive sides of the business. If anyone understands the broad sweep of creative communications in the twenty-first century it's Nick.

....

save multiple versions of your file in case you need to go back; the chances are you never will. As Mark Twain said,

"Eliminate every third word. It gives your writing a remarkable vigor."

You also need to make sure what you're saying is true. Your words could be supremely elegant yet complete fiction. Unless you're making a virtue of hyperbole or your tone is obviously light-hearted (both perfectly good approaches, by the way) then whatever you write has to be scrupulously honest. Either stick to the facts, or depart from them with such chutzpah that no one in their right mind could mistake your piece for the truth.

Finally, if a good idea gets rejected by your client/boss then stash it away in your bottom drawer in the sure and certain knowledge that another opportunity to use it will come along sooner or later. Probably sooner. It's amazing how often ideas created for one task can find a home in another—and because you've already done the difficult thinking part you'll be able to produce them in record time, making you look super-efficient and eminently promotion-worthy.

....

Now you have a go

It won't have escaped your notice there's plenty of poor writing out there—confused, over-complex, and under-stimulating. Of course you'd never create anything like that, and now's your chance to prove it.

Workout One

Find a piece of copy that really makes your toes curl, then write a short analysis of why it's so bad—a couple of paragraphs is enough. Justify your criticism as objectively as possible. The copy you choose can come from any source—packaging, ad, website, brochure, and so on. To keep things simple, pick something reasonably brief—say under 100 words.

Next, write one clear, strong sentence or phrase that describes what you think the original is trying to say. This should be the absolute essence of the message.

Finally, use the ideas and techniques covered in this lesson to write a new and improved version of the original, based on the essence you've just identified.

The aim here is threefold: Find rational reasons to back up your instincts (something you'll be required to do in conversations and meetings on a regular basis), sensitize yourself to what a piece of text is *really* trying to say, and practice improving the work of others.

Workout Two

Plenty of real-world copywriting isn't writing at all, it's editing and reworking existing text. To get you comfortable in this role we want you to redraft the following chunk of copy—taken from a fictional airline print ad—in one of the structures we suggested earlier:

- Issues>implications>actions
- Past>present>future
- Context>analysis>conclusion>actions
- Issue>background>current situation>conclusion>suggestions
- Problem>solution>results
- Inverted triangle
- Goal>step one>step two>step X>result
- Q&A

Feel free to add and subtract details as you see fit. The aim is to build your confidence working with existing text, not scrupulously stick to the source material.

With great service, great food and great in-flight entertainment, we've made flying to the Far East more enjoyable than you thought possible.

There's no reason why a long flight should be short on luxury. That's why our seats are the comfiest in their class, with a massive 35in of space between rows so you'll arrive at your destination relaxed and ready to enjoy your stay.

The soothing atmosphere isn't just down to the seating— fabulous food and fine wines play their part, with menus designed by Andrew Walker, owner of Shanghai's fabulous Starpool restaurant.

Then there's our award-winning "100% Entertainment" system, featuring 10 movie channels, 12 TV channels (including Nickelodeon), 20 computer games, and 15 music stations with everything from classical to club hits. Your channel controller even doubles as the world's first in-flight phone so you can let your friends know you're having the time of your life.

However you look at it, flying with us is a truly elevating experience.

Lesson Three:
Making the Magic Happen

Memes, memory, and sticky lines

Some ads take hold and won't let go.

In the last lesson we explained how to create good, strong copy. In this companion lesson we look at how to add memorability to your messages. As we've said, the two lessons work together to cover the basics and beyond.

We'll begin with an anecdote from the distant past, and that means switching to the first person as Roger takes the writing reins.

It's the early seventies. A small boy (Rog) and his even smaller brother (Tim) are sitting in front of the family's recently acquired color telly enjoying pre-dinner cartoons. The ads come on and suddenly we're confronted by a group of colorful metallic robot-type creatures sitting round a table in what must surely be a spaceship. That got our attention. Then the metalheads start to speak and it just gets better.

Martian One (some sort of leader): "On your last trip, did you discover what the Earth people eat?"

Martian Two (some sort of explorer): "They eat a great many of these." [Holds up a potato in his unfeasibly crude claw. The other Martians immediately start chattering among themselves.]

"They peel them with their metal knives…" [Chattering steps up a pace.]

"…boil them for 20 of their minutes…" [Metallic laughter begins to displace the chattering.]

"…then they smash them all to bits." [Martians overcome with laughter.]

Martian One: "They are clearly a most primitive people." [Whole group collapse into fits of laughter, some rolling around and waving their arms in the air.]

Slogan (sung): "For mash, get Smash."

We thought we'd died and gone to heaven. Remember, this is just a few years after the first moon landing, and all things space/UFO/alien-related were big news in our playground.

Now, impressive though the Martians were, it wasn't these crudely animated aliens that really made us chuckle; it was their dialogue. I can repeat the script even now (in fact I wrote most of the above from memory). We chanted it, repeated it, reveled in it. Our parents' refusal to put us up for adoption after hearing

The Sugar Puffs Honey Monster, another of John Webster's cool creations.

"They are clearly a most primitive people HAHAHA" for the thousandth time as they struggled to get dinner ready is a testament to their patience and parenting skills. Even more remarkable is why these words have stuck with me for so many years. But stuck they have.

Although this little tale is intensely personal, it's also universal; we all have similar stories featuring lines of copy we picked up in our past and carry around with us as part of who we are. Taken from print and TV ads, packaging, posters, and public information films, they've stuck with us—stuck to us—as some of our most persistent memories. They are sticky lines, and they are the subject of this lesson.

Ear-catching language in action.

What is this "sticky" of which we speak?

Let's properly define "sticky lines," a phrase borrowed from the online world, where it is used to refer to compelling content intended to keep a user glued to a particular website.

For our purposes a "sticky line" is any headline, slogan, tagline, and so on that lodges in its audience's brains and refuses to budge. Sticky lines tend to appear at the top or bottom of a piece of communication, although the principles explained here work equally well for any compressed text in any location—captions, conclusions, summaries, e-mail subject lines, etc.

Copy that achieves sticky status tends to exhibit certain qualities. These have been understood— with varying degrees of clarity and with changing emphasis—for many years. As proof let's go back to 1955; "Rock Around the Clock" has just been released, the first Disneyland has recently opened in California, and a new board game called Scrabble is proving quite a success. In the US an advertising executive called Charles Whittier has published a book called *Creative Advertising*. In it he defines a slogan as:

> *...a statement of such merit about a product or service that it is worthy of continuous repetition in advertising, is worthwhile for the public to remember, and is phrased in such a way that the public is likely to remember it.*

In other words a slogan (or in our case, a sticky line) is *worth repeating*, *worth remembering*, and—crucially— is *written in a way that makes it memorable*.

Now whizz forward 50 years to the new millennium. UK adman Dave Trott had this to say in an article for the UK's *Campaign* magazine:

> *"A slogan is there to deliver a USP or branding. If you love my commercial you shouldn't be able to describe it to anyone else without mentioning the name of the product and the slogan."*

In other words a sticky line should be integral to a piece of communication and not stuck on as an ear-pleasing afterthought. In the same article Andrew Cracknell, executive creative director for a veritable alphabet soup of international advertising agencies

including FCB, WCRS, and APL, adds:

> *The ones that stick out tend to be written in the public language. There has to be rhythm or a rhyme or a quirkiness in the line that catches the ear.*

"Catching the ear"—that's stickiness in three words. The examples Cracknell offers are "It's a lot less bovver than a hover," "Vorsprung durch Technik," and "Beanz Meanz Heinz"—all of which do indeed show plenty of rhythm, rhyme, and quirk. We could add Nike's "Just do it," Bic Lighter's "Flick your Bic," Ford's "Everything we do is driven by you," and eBay's "Buy it. Sell it. Love it."

Having outlined the qualities of a sticky line in broad terms, let's look at memorability in more detail.

Memes mean Heinz

Sorry, we couldn't resist that. Allow us to explain. In his groundbreaking book *The Selfish Gene*, Oxford University biologist Richard Dawkins introduced the world to a powerful new idea: the meme (rhymes with "seem," as if you didn't know).

A meme, Dawkins wrote, is much like its biological cousin the gene. Like a gene, a meme is a self-replicating unit of information. However, memes don't replicate biologically; instead they're passed around in the form of ideas. Dawkins described memes as the "basic unit of cultural transmission." He notes:

"Just as genes propagate themselves by moving from body to body via sperm or eggs, so memes propagate themselves by moving from brain to brain via culture."

Let's have some examples. Presumably at some point in your life you've had a song going round and round in your head for hours on end, driving you slowly insane? That tune is a meme in action. Or you've heard a catchphrase on a comedy show and found yourself unconsciously using it? Another meme. It's the same with any fashion, idea, or image that finds its way into our collective consciousness and spreads like wildfire. Very crudely, we could say a meme is any cultural expression that suddenly seems to be everywhere.

These examples illustrate why the much-maligned meme is sometimes called an *idea virus* (or in the case of music, an *ear worm*). Much work has been done mapping the spread of memes in culture, and the dynamic they follow is indeed that of contagion. Like real viruses, memes are self-perpetuating and almost impossible to eradicate. It's no exaggeration to say cultures catch memes in much the same way populations catch colds.

Given their infectious quality it's not surprising that memes are at the heart of what has become known—appropriately enough—as "viral marketing," a loose collection of techniques designed to piggyback on existing social relationships or networks to sell or promote something. The classic form is word-of-mouth recommendation—either face-to-face or online—but any easily shareable content does much the same job.

Viral has become a crucial part of marketing practice, and underpins such wildly successful ad campaigns as Burger King's "Subservient Chicken," Cadbury's "Drumming Gorilla," and Old Spice's remarkable "The

Blackpool's rather incredible Comedy Carpet. Created by artist Gordon Young and designed by Why Not Associates, this typographic tour de force contains 160,000 precisely cut granite letters embedded in concrete, spelling out the jokes and catchphrases of over 1,000 of the UK's best-loved entertainers. The result is 23,000 square feet of comedy memes.

Man Your Man Could Smell Like." The latter attracted almost 7 million YouTube views in just 24 hours, rising to 23 million views in just 36 hours. Needless to say, all three owe a good dollop of their success to their meme-like nature. In fact it shouldn't be called viral marketing at all—it's *meme* marketing, pure and simple.

Hopefully you can see how relevant memes are to the subject of stickiness. Robin Wight—the W in ad agency WCRS and a colorful creative like they just don't make any more—is a big fan of memes. He told us:

"As copywriters we're basically meme men. We want to infect people's brains with our brands, and things that have got some memetic quality are more easily caught by the brain. Memes are memory devices that help spread words from brain to brain."

All of which reinforces what we said earlier: If you want your ideas to spread and stick, make them meme-y.

Now, important though memes are, the last pages simply make explicit something that good copywriters have understood instinctively for decades—that certain ideas, expressed in certain ways, have dramatically more sticking power than others. And it's to those "certain ideas" and "certain ways" that we now turn.

Because I'm worth it   Just do it
Think different
Every little helps   The best a man can get
Does exactly what it says on the tin
I'm lovin' it   Keep calm and carry on
Naughty but nice
It could be you   The appliance of science
It's good to talk

Twelve ad slogans that have entered everyday language in the UK—perhaps the ultimate form of stickiness.

How to make your copy stick

To become truly sticky, a piece of copy needs to be *simple*, it needs to *give pleasure*, and it needs to be *easily passed on*. If a potential meme/sticky line isn't instantly intelligible then the chances are it won't catch its audience's ear. If it doesn't provide a moment of enjoyment then there's no motivation for someone to make the meme their own or share it with others, and if it isn't easily transferable—either in speech, writing, or via a social network—then it's destined for a short, obscure life.

What follows is a toolbox of techniques intended to help you make your messages simple, pleasurable, and transferable. Refer to them when you're next stuck for a bit of stickiness—they don't tell you what to say (how could they?), but they do tell you some proven ways to say it.

Create an emotional connection

Sticky writing touches the reader. This connection comes from making it personal. In fact a prime way to make a line sticky is to help readers see themselves in it. According to Robin Wight:

> *The way to get me to read 5,000 words of copy is to have a headline all about Robin Wight. The more you can make an ad personally relevant to its reader, the more chance you have of getting through.*

Say it strange

Why did Apple say "Think different" and not "Think differently"? Why did they follow it with "The funnest iPod ever" rather than something like "The most enjoyable iPod we've ever made"? Why does Aleksandr the meerkat—spokesanimal for price-comparison website comparethemarket.com—say "Simples" and not "Simple"? Why did 7UP promote itself as "The Uncola"? Why did Budweiser decide "Whasssup?" was the perfect way to build their brand? We'll tell you why: They're all examples of a linguistic quirk used to create a mighty meme. By twisting language just a bit they achieved maximum memorability. It's a powerful technique but be warned, it's easy to get wrong.

Aleksandr says "Simples."

Budman says "Whassup!"

IS YOUR LIFE MORE INTERESTING THAN A SQUIRREL'S?

You might think it is. But you take the same tube everyday. You spend five days a week sitting at your desk, work through lunch and stay late. You buy the same sandwich day in, day out with the same drink. You make excuses not to see friends at weekends because 'you're busy' when you're really just watching TV. Sunday is spent recovering from Saturday and preparing for Monday. It doesn't sound too exciting does it? Learn from the squirrel. He lives in the Royal Parks. His commute is a playful skip through beautiful gardens surrounding vast lakes. His office is some 5,000 acres of striking parkland. He spends time with his family and his only deadline is winter. He eats nuts but not because Nigella says so. His home has historic landscapes alongside beautiful fountains and he doesn't pay a penny. Now who's nuts?

Jaunty copy that highlights a fact many of us would rather not acknowledge: Our lives are less interesting than a squirrel's.

The brand managers for Birds Eye Potato Waffles clearly felt they could do the same with their slogan "They're waffly versatile." The result is truly waffle.

Tell them something they don't know

A good way to create stickiness is to offer your reader relevant, thought-provoking information. Ogilvy's classic ad that begins "At 60 miles an hour the loudest noise in this new Rolls-Royce comes from the electric clock" is a marvelous example (see overleaf), as he went on to support this imagination-grabbing headline with a slew of interesting info-nuggets.

Ogilvy's ad ran way back in 1958, yet its approach is entirely usable today. In recent years Roger used the same "give 'em something interesting to think about" technique in a brochure for ultra-high-end cell phone brand Vertu, listing 55 rock-solid reasons to believe the hype.

Tell them a story

We cover this in more detail in Lesson Six, but the important thing to know is good stories hold people's attention in a way little else can. We don't mean "Once upon a time"; we mean any narrative that creates a sense of involvement and identification. If readers can project themselves into your story then the chances are they'll stay with you to the end and remember what you said.

Have something to say

In his book *The Craft of Copywriting*, UK adman Alastair Crompton points out that there are only two kinds of ad: those with something to say and, er, those that don't. Sticky ads—and indeed sticky texts of all descriptions —are very much the former. If you've got something intelligent, beneficial, or interesting to say about your product, service, or brand then *for God's sake say it*. You'd be amazed how many organizations clog their communications with irrelevant puffery instead of emphasizing their real point of difference. And don't bury what you've got to say in your body copy—get it up top in the headline or lead paragraph. Now is not the time for modesty.

THE VILLAGE GROCER

The Rolls-Royce Silver Cloud—$13,550.

"At 60 miles an hour the loudest noise in this new Rolls-Royce comes from the electric clock"

What *makes* Rolls-Royce the best car in the world? "There is really no magic about it—
it is merely patient attention to detail," says an eminent Rolls-Royce engineer.

1. "At 60 miles an hour the loudest noise comes from the electric clock," reports the Technical Editor of THE MOTOR. The silence of the engine is uncanny. Three mufflers tune out sound frequencies—acoustically.

2. Every Rolls-Royce engine is run for seven hours at full throttle before installation, and each car is test-driven for hundreds of miles over varying road surfaces.

3. The Rolls-Royce is designed as an *owner-driven* car. It is eighteen inches shorter than the largest domestic cars.

4. The car has power steering, power brakes and automatic gear-shift. It is very easy to drive and to park. No chauffeur required.

5. There is no metal-to-metal contact between the body of the car and the chassis frame—except for the speedometer drive. The entire body is insulated and under-sealed.

6. The finished car spends a week in the final test-shop, being fine-tuned. Here it is subjected to ninety-eight separate ordeals. For example, the engineers use a *stethoscope* to listen for axle-whine.

7. The Rolls-Royce is guaranteed for *three years*. With a new network of dealers and parts-depots from

Coast to Coast, service is no longer any problem.

8. The famous Rolls-Royce radiator has never been changed, except that when Sir Henry Royce died in 1933 the monogram RR was changed from red to black.

9. The coachwork is given five coats of primer paint, and hand rubbed between each coat, before *fourteen* coats of finishing paint go on.

10. By moving a switch on the steering column, you can adjust the shock-absorbers to suit road conditions. (The lack of fatigue in driving this car is remarkable.)

11. Another switch defrosts the rear window, by heating a network of 1360 invisible wires in the glass. There are two separate ventilating systems, so that you can ride in comfort with all the windows closed. Air conditioning is optional.

12. The seats are upholstered with eight hides of English leather—enough to make 128 pairs of soft shoes.

13. A picnic table, veneered in French walnut, slides out from under the dash. Two more swing out behind the front seats.

14. You can get such optional extras as an Espresso coffee-making machine, a dictating machine, a bed, hot and cold water for washing, an electric razor.

15. You can lubricate the entire chassis by simply pushing a pedal from the driver's seat. A gauge on the dash shows the level of oil in the crankcase.

16. Gasoline consumption is remarkably low and there is no need to use premium gas; a happy economy.

17. There are two separate systems of power brakes, hydraulic and mechanical. The Rolls-Royce is a very *safe* car—and also a very *lively* car. It cruises serenely at eighty-five. Top speed is in excess of 100 m.p.h.

18. Rolls-Royce engineers make periodic visits to inspect owners' motor cars and advise on service.

ROLLS-ROYCE AND BENTLEY

19. The Bentley is made by Rolls-Royce. Except for the radiators, they are identical motor cars, manufactured by the same engineers in the same works. The Bentley costs $300 less, because its radiator is simpler to make. People who feel diffident about driving a Rolls-Royce can buy a Bentley.

PRICE. The car illustrated in this advertisement—f.o.b. principal port of entry—costs $13,550.

If you would like the rewarding experience of driving a Rolls-Royce or Bentley, get in touch with our dealer. His name is on the bottom of this page. Rolls-Royce Inc., 10 Rockefeller Plaza, New York, N.Y.

JET ENGINES AND THE FUTURE

Certain airlines have chosen Rolls-Royce turbo-jets for their Boeing 707's and Douglas DC8's. Rolls-Royce prop-jets are in the Vickers Viscount, the Fairchild F.27 and the Grumman Gulfstream.

Rolls-Royce engines power more than half the turbo-jet and prop-jet airliners supplied to or on order for world airlines.

Rolls-Royce now employ 42,000 people and the company's engineering experience does not stop at motor cars and jet engines. There are Rolls-Royce diesel and gasoline engines for many other applications.

The huge research and development resources of the company are now at work on many projects for the future, including nuclear and rocket propulsion.

Special showing of the Rolls-Royce and Bentley at Salter Automotive Imports, Inc., 9009 Carnegie Ave., tomorrow through April 26.

For winemaker Primi Piatti,
every bottle tells a story.

You just sat down
to a blind date

She says she's the
settle-down,
get-married type

You ask to take
your food and the
wine away in a
doggy bag

You're sitting opposite
the love of your life

She's got news for you

You're going to be
a father

She says you're going
to be a father

She says you're going
to be a father

She says you're going
to be a father

You're staring at
the in-laws
over lunch

You remember not
to mention the war

You make some
silly joke

They laugh politely

You remember not
to mention the war

You're remarking
how great the
food is

You're exchanging
bites

And laughs

You've mentioned
the war

Quick, order
another bottle

© 1962 VOLKSWAGEN OF AMERICA, INC.

Think small.

Our little car isn't so much of a novelty any more.

A couple of dozen college kids don't try to squeeze inside it.

The guy at the gas station doesn't ask where the gas goes.

Nobody even stares at our shape.

In fact, some people who drive our little flivver don't even think 32 miles to the gallon is going any great guns.

Or using five pints of oil instead of five quarts.

Or never needing anti-freeze.

Or racking up 40,000 miles on a set of tires.

That's because once you get used to some of our economies, you don't even think about them any more.

Except when you squeeze into a small parking spot. Or renew your small insurance. Or pay a small repair bill. Or trade in your old VW for a new one.

Think it over.

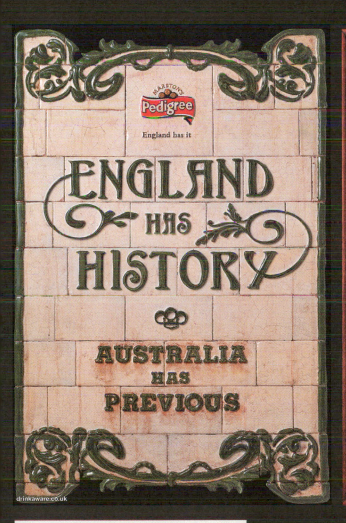

Two lovely "compare and contrast" ads for Pedigree Bitter. The tone is pure pub banter.

Granny Smiths.

What's the difference between ours and our competitors'?

Not much really.

They're the same quality as Waitrose.

And the same price as Asda.

There's an appealing restraint to this that gives the selling point a sugar coating.

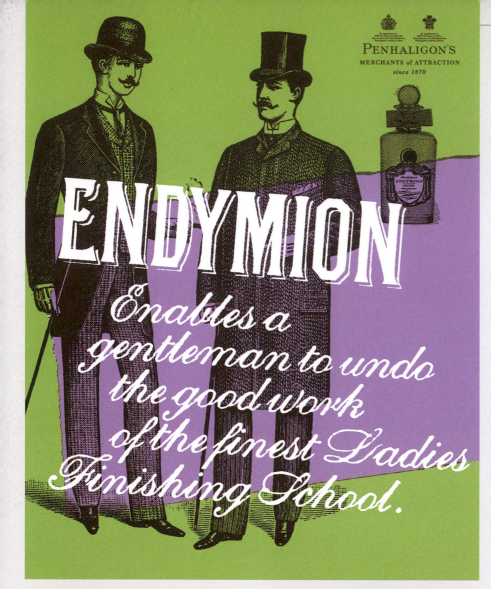

PENHALIGON'S
MERCHANTS of ATTRACTION
since 1870

ENDYMION

Enables a gentleman to undo the good work of the finest Ladies Finishing School.

MALABAH

Perfect for any young lady looking to find herself compromised.

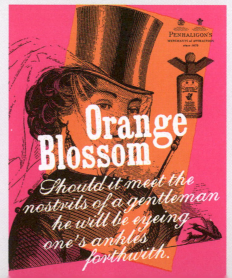

Orange Blossom

Should it meet the nostrils of a gentleman he will be eyeing one's ankles forthwith.

Three examples of product as benefit from Penhaligon. The ad on the left here is a classy take on the classic angle that aftershave makes its wearer more attractive.

A different approach to proving it. Not a number in sight, but this digital before-and-after promo piece for a freelance proofreader is equally effective.

Paul Dalling
Independent Proofreader

"To be or to be: that is the question." Or is it? Most readers won't have spotted the missing word in that first sentence. That's where a good proofreader come in.

Paul Dalling is a god proofreader. He's spent a lifetime working in the print industry, proofreading everything from goverment reports to exam paper's, high security documents, websites and colanders.

Proofreading
Proofreading covers the usual checking for spelling, typographical, punctuation, and grammatical errors. (Spell-check has its uses but it only catch so mulch and will thin a sentience like this is fine.)

Editing
As well as proofreading, Paul will check the text from a stylistic point of view to introduce an enhanced reader experience in terms of clarity and consistency issues.

Fact checking
Wherever necessary, Paul will check the factual accuracy and relevance of your content and suggest rewording. He is one of the best in the world at this.

Service
Paul will work on hard copy manuscripts sent by post or e-mailed files using the 'track changes' function in Microsoft Word®.

Fees
Fees are negotiable and reflect the nature of the work. Straight forward proofreading starts at £7 per 1000 words. Bear in mind that the cost of not proofreading (reprints, lost custom, damaged crudibility) is often much greater.

To call or to email
01332 664439
typo@pauldalling.co.uk

CLICK TO VIEW THE TYPOS...

Paul Dalling
Independent Proofreader

"To be or to be: that is the question." Or is it? Most readers won't have spotted the missing word in that first sentence. That's where a good proofreader come in.   s

Paul Dalling is a god proofreader. He's spent   o
a lifetime working in the print industry, proofreading everything from goverment   n
reports to exam paper's, high security documents, websites and colanders.   calendars.

Proofreading
Proofreading covers the usual checking for spelling, typographical, punctuation, and grammatical errors. (Spell-check has its uses but it only catch so mulch and will thin a sentience like this is fine.)   es

Editing
As well as proofreading, Paul will check the text from a stylistic point of view to introduce an enhanced reader experience in terms of clarity and consistency issues!   greater clarity and consistency.

Fact checking
Wherever necessary, Paul will check the factual accuracy and relevance of your content and suggest rewording. He is one of the best in the world at this!   STET

Service
Paul will work on hard copy manuscripts sent by post or e-mailed files using the 'track changes' function in Microsoft Word®.

Fees
Fees are negotiable and reflect the nature of the work. Straight forward proofreading starts at £7 per 1000 words. Bear in mind that the cost of not proofreading (reprints, lost custom, damaged crudibility) is often much greater.   credibility

To call or to email
01332 664439
typo@pauldalling.co.uk   GO BACK TO THE ORIGINAL COPY

Bear in mind your message doesn't need to be that insightful, it just needs to act as the foundation for the rest of your argument. As Dave Trott puts it:

Think of an oyster. You start out with a piece of grit, and build a pearl around it. People buy the pearl, not the grit. But no grit, no pearl.

Compare and contrast

Seven-stone weakling into hard-bodied he-man. Filth-stained frock into dazzling dress. Smoker's teeth into sparkling incisors. You get the idea—it's before and after, and it works. It may sound a tired technique, but it's as tired as you make it. There's *always* a fresh angle when it comes to dramatizing the benefit, and it's your job to find it. Faster, slower, bigger, smaller, reassuringly expensive, remarkably cheap—the list goes on. To be effective and to avoid accusations of cynicism you need to compare like with like and only draw conclusions that can be justified. Do that and you're only doing what any sensible purchaser does when sizing up a product or service, so why not help them on their way?

BUFFALO BILL'S WILD WEST   25.

EXT. GOLDVILLE - DAY

A dry and sunny day. A ghost town in the Old Far West. We see a cowboy shooting.
He reloads the gun. We see an outsider approaching. He's shot, but doesn't fall off
his horse. He's alive. The outsider gets off his horse. He leads it to the old smelly
stables, hides and leans against the animal, trying not to collapse, but he's weak. The
outsider tries not to stumble. He's dizzy. Exhausted, he tries to stop his bleeding.
He ties his leg and he drags himself to the abandoned workshop. His life is on the
line. He gets to the high street. Then he walks towards the center to hide, and stops
right in front of the saloon. He takes off his hat. Losing his strength, he dies.

            BAD DOG

    Finally. Huh. Now, this damned stinking insect won't bother no
    one no more.... Son of a gun. He's in hell now.

            SHERIFF

    That's right. We gotta leave this damned place now. Before them vultures
    get here.

INT. SALOON - DAY

The saloon is dark. The cowboy orders a cold bourbon with his gun in his hand.
A lot of people talk. The sheriff slowly turns away and sneaks up behind the cowboy
who can't see, when the barman hands the cold drink over to the drunk cowboy.
The cowboy lifts it with his hands shaking and then makes a toast. That's when the
sheriff approaches the cowboy, without hesitation, pulls his left arm back and
handcuffs him, then gets the big glass and drinks, mocking the cowboy. And spits
in the same glass of bourbon. Suddenly everyone hears some loud shots outside.
It is two outsiders fighting over a woman.

            SMOKIN' KID AND BILL

    Hands up, everybody on the floor right now. This is a robbery...

The rope around her wrists dug deeper into her skin with every attempt she made to free herself. She stopped, covered in cold sweat, her wrists shredded. She heard the girls laughing on the other side of the wall. If only she could make them hear her, but that filthy rag in her mouth would smother any cry. Besides, everything was drowned out by the overly enthusiastic sports commentator on the TV in the corner. She stared around the room and tried to discover a way out, but the dark was thick and impenetrable.

It could never be long before he'd be back to continue his interrogation. How long could she keep on telling him she knew nothing of Sara's hiding place? Stumbling sounds, the doorknob moved. The yellow light from the hall lashed into the room and showed his silhouette in the doorway. This was her only chance to get out. In a sudden outburst that contained all her anger, she stormed at the door, still bound to her chair. If you've had the time to read this story this far, you'd better try the train sometime. Dutch Railways. Come along.

Leaving aside the distinct possibility of driver distraction and ensuing highway mayhem, this text makes its point—that if you can read this you must be stuck in traffic—with wit and intelligence.

A brilliant combination of design and copy that graphically illustrates how widescreen gives you more.

Prove it

One of the all-time top techniques for creating stickiness. If possible, *explain the benefit of your product or service using specific numbers*. If you've picked the right angle, and your figures are sufficiently impressive, then stickiness will ensue. The other way to say this is, "Don't claim, demonstrate" (or if you prefer, "facts persuade"). In each case the sentiment is the same: provide objective proof to substantiate what you're saying and you'll get through to people.

Don't play it safe

You've been asked to write an in-box leaflet for some new running shoes. Most folks who buy them will jog around their local park, perspiring lightly while trying to look cool. But you don't write this. While doing the detailed research we recommended in the last lesson you discover this particular sneaker is favored by some ultramarathon madman who achieves distances normally associated with airliners. *That's* what you write about. The unstated message is: If this shoe works for him, just think what it'll do for you. So try describing your subject overcoming the toughest challenge imaginable—the so-called torture test. That should create a bit of stick.

Translation: "This car works when it's virtually submerged, so think how it'll perform on dry land."

ALARM GOES OFF. SNOOZE GOES ON. ALARM GOES OFF. DRESSING GOWN GOES ON. SHOWER GOES ON. SHOWER GOES OFF. TEETH ARE CLEANED. CLOTHES IRONED. HAIR BRUSHED. LUNCH MADE. LUNCH DROPPED. LUNCH IS MADE AGAIN. BAGS ARE PACKED. LOVED ONES ARE KISSED. HOME IS LEFT. THE JOURNEY BEGINS. HEADPHONES IN. EYE CONTACT AVOIDED. OXFORD STREET IS REACHED. DESTINATION IN SIGHT. THE HANDLE IS PULLED. THE HANDLE IS PULLED. THE HANDLE IS PULLED. THE HANDLE IS PUSHED. BARISTAS ARE MUMBLED TO. COFFEE IS POURED. REGULAR SEAT IS FOUND. YOUR CUP IS LIFTED. THE INDELIBLY RICH AND LUXURIOUS FLAT WHITE COFFEE REACHES THE BACK OF YOUR THROAT, WARMING YOU DOWN TO THE FARTHEST REACHES OF YOUR BODY AS THE CAFFEINE SURGES THROUGH YOU LIKE THE SMOOTHEST, MOST VELVETY HOMING MISSILE KNOWN TO MAN.

YOU WAKE.

COSTA OXFORD STREET. WE MAKE IT BETTER EVERY MORNING

Pure "slice of life" copy for one of the UK's biggest coffee chains. Every nod or smile of recognition adds to its stickiness. Note the

PLEASE BUCKLE UP FOR SECURITY

We brake for fish.

How can we call that mud-splattered vehicle beautiful? Quite easily, actually.

The Range Rover was not only exhibited at the Louvre, it's also a favourite of fashionable drivers from St. Moritz to Milan.

And with its Land Rover pedigree, it's a favourite on the Serengeti and in the Outback, as well.

In addition to its 4-wheel drive, its Differential Lock provides grip enough for a blizzard or bog.

It can also see you readily across terrain as rough as this.

RANGE ROVER

And with its fuel injected V-8 engine, the Range Rover even excels on the surface that most challenges most rugged 4x4s: A paved road.

What's more, its standard equipment includes all the luxury features you'd expect in a vehicle priced just north of $30,000.

So why not call 1-800 123-4567 for a dealer convenient to you?

After all, the uglier driving gets, the more beautiful a Range Rover becomes.

Stephen Leslie

Don't do it. Stop now before you get the bug. Go find yourself a proper job. I say this entirely seriously (also selfishly—there's enough competition out there already and the last thing I need are more people trying to steal my work).

Write quickly. There will be plenty of time to revise and rewrite later. Try to invest your work with energy.

Aldous Huxley wrote something to the effect that mankind will not be defeated by the tyranny of any government but instead will invent ways to distract itself to death. Huxley was anticipating the Internet and its hideous ability to sabotage your carefully structured working day. If you want to write, log off.

Love your first draft but don't love it too much. Even if it's perfect the powers that be will demand rewrites because they can, so practice holding some stuff back. Remember, it's not so much about writing as rewriting. The sooner you understand this, the better.

Learn to cut your own stuff. I guarantee you will be asked (or ordered) to cut lines that you adore. So learn to self-cut. In the long run it's less painful.

It's an unhealthy and lonely vocation so try to get up and walk about a bit or go for a run. Better still, try going for a walk or a run with another writer. You can moan to each other.

Read other writers' work. That's the best way to learn about writing.

Take notes. People say great, unscripted things all the time. Use them.

You will constantly be asked "What else have you got?," so it helps to have an answer. Learn to juggle. Keep multiple balls in the air. Spin many plates. Always have a fall-back. Don't put all your eggs in one basket. Oh, and avoid clichés.

Steal a bit but not too much. Try to learn the difference between a clever new take on something and a blatant rip-off.

Ignore most advice given to you by other writers. We are a savage and bitter breed who love the sound of our own voices and delight in the misery of others.

....

Stephen Leslie worked as a script reader, tea maker, cameraman, producer, and director. He started out as a script reader for Sally Potter, John Schlesinger, and Jon Amiel. He then wrote and directed an award-winning short film about bestiality and royalty called *I Was Catherine the Great's Stable Boy*. This helped win him a place on the BBC's Trainee Assistant Producer scheme, after which he spent four years directing documentaries for the BBC. For the last ten years he has focused almost exclusively on scriptwriting, with commissions from the BBC, Film4, Working Title, Revolution, and Qwerty. Back in 2007 he was (perhaps prematurely) named a Screen International "Star of Tomorrow."

....

Keep it real

Concrete, tangible ideas tend to engage readers
more readily than their abstract, intangible
equivalents—it's just easier for the casual reader to
see what's in it for them. Most modern business-speak
falls into this trap, with "core competencies" instead of
"skills" and "proactive strategies" rather than "plans."
As the business writer John Simmons puts it,
"Language that speaks of real people doing real
things creates images that lodge more deeply and
stay longer in our memories," which is a nice way of
describing stickiness.

How to check
for stickiness

The only real test of stickiness is the extent to which
a line embeds itself in the minds of its audience.
Nevertheless, here are a few questions you can use to
make sure you're on track.

Is it surprising?

If the reader can all but finish your sentences for
you then no, it isn't surprising, and no, it won't be
sticky. Taking an unexpected approach—particularly
in situations where conventions rule—will give your
writing more glue. One simple and highly recommended
way to do this is to start your piece a couple of sentences
into your argument. Write as you normally would,
then try deleting the first one or two (or more)
sentences. By removing the usual preamble
you'll create a jolt that will grab readers' attention.
Just throw them into the narrative and let
them figure it out.

With a surprising headline like this we can't
help but be curious about the rest.

volkswagen.co.uk/efficiency

~~Our~~ BlueMotion ~~range combines lighter materials, enhanced aerodynamics, economical engines and tyres that create less friction, which~~ saves you ~~fuel and can reduce your tax, which means you will have more~~ money.

volkswagen.co.uk/efficiency

DSG is our clever gearbox which has two separate clutches. With the 7-speed Direct Shift Gearbox, each change can be practically seamless, which helps save a lot of energy. So not only do you get smooth acceleration, but you also use less fuel.*

The highlights/non-crossed-out-bits spell out the "So what?" Two messages in one.

Not just what it is, but how to use it.

Would you want to hang out with this copy for South African accessories company Musica? Maybe—it'd certainly be a night to remember (assuming you survived).

Does it pass the "As opposed to what?" test?

A surprising number of organizations promote themselves using lines that don't stand up to scrutiny. To avoid this, always ask yourself, "As opposed to what?" UK bank NatWest currently uses the tagline "Helpful banking"—as opposed to what, *un*helpful banking? If what you say is obviously desirable then it won't achieve cut-through—it's just what any reasonable person would expect. Trying to make a virtue of a necessity can even sound a little desperate. Readers of a skeptical disposition (roughly 99 percent) might well respond, "Jeez, is that the best they can say about themselves?"

Does it pass the "So what?" test?

If your words are underwhelming then they're unlikely to stick. The solution is to ask "So what?" This simple question is a brutally effective way of rooting out weak thinking. If the answer is a deafening silence or shrug of the shoulders then you're off-target. Yes it's cruel, but then so are audiences if they suspect their time is being wasted. What we're suggesting is that everything you say has to have some reason to exist, usually connected to your audience and their wants and needs. Pointless puffery may fill the page but it drains audience interest faster than you can say "flannel."

I'm sorry London.

For all the women I have tortured, maimed and killed. I was cold, heartless and indiscriminate. I did not care who I hurt. Sometimes I attacked with speed. Other times I'd hide for years, waiting patiently before I surfaced. And while some escaped, the fear of me lived on in their lives. I thought I was unstoppable. I tore families apart, fed on fear, revelled in the carnage that I created. But no more. Now the fear is all mine. Now I'm the one under constant attack. I am suffering the way I have made others suffer. And now I know how it feels, I admit it London, I'm scared. I'm getting weaker. Losing this battle. I don't expect forgiveness. I just needed you to know before I die.

BREAKTHROUGH.ORG.UK

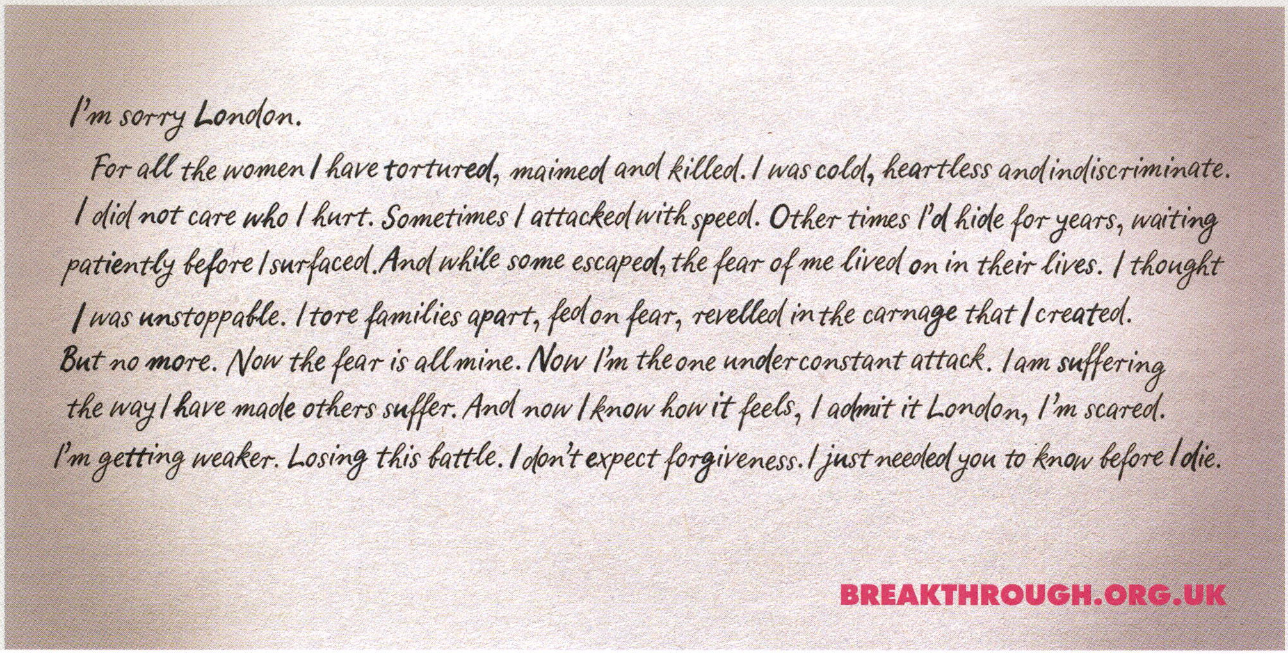

Has it got real personality?

As so often in our line of work, it pays to compare what we write to people. The ones we're attracted to tend to have the most appealing personalities. So one important question to ask is, "How personable is my work? If it were a person, would I be drawn to him/her or run a mile?" If your prose is the textual equivalent of a railfan with radioactive halitosis then clearly it needs more work. Your readers don't have to fall in love with your on-page personality, they just have to avoid being actively repelled.

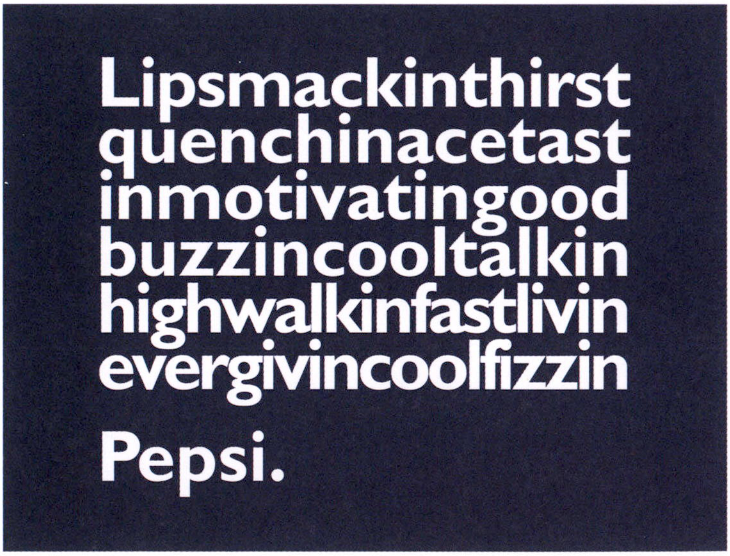

Lipsmackinthirst quenchinacetast inmotivatingood buzzincooltalkin highwalkinfastlivin evergivincoolfizzin

Pepsi.

Classic pleasing-to-read copy from the Other Cola.

Simon Veksner

There's an important concept that (bizarrely, in my opinion) hardly anyone ever talks about when it comes to writing for advertising: emotion.

We all know that human beings are primarily emotionally driven, and that rational stuff doesn't really motivate us at the most profound level. It's just a thin veneer we pretend to have, to stop ourselves stealing other people's cars and women.

Unfortunately, the rational stuff is usually what gets put in briefs—and in articles about how to write copy.

Nearly all the advice I see about writing headlines and taglines talks about how to make them impactful and memorable, using rhetorical devices like repetition (the US Army's "Be all that you can be"), reversal ("Our food is fresh. Our customers are spoiled."), rhyme (wartime slogan "Loose lips sink ships"), and alliteration (Brylcreem's "A little dab'll do ya").

They never talk about freighting a line with an emotional payload, the thing that would make it truly powerful.

The FedEx tagline "When it absolutely, positively has to be there overnight" is undoubtedly a clever turn of phrase. But what makes it great is that it also captures the emotion of the package-sender—their desire for certainty. It's this emotional content that elevates the best lines beyond being mere clever wordplay. After all, advertising is seduction...and without emotion, seduction won't succeed.

After graduating from Oxford with a degree in philosophy and french, Simon had a brief and unsuccessful career as an investment banker. He then tried journalism, writing articles for women's magazines about what men "really" like in bed. Finally he settled on advertising, and was a creative director at BBH in London and DDB in Sydney, before starting his own agency in 2012. His blog—Scamp—became the most popular ad blog in the UK and led to a book deal, with *How to Make It as an Advertising Creative* published in May 2010. Recently Simon has been crowdsourcing ads to promote atheism. As he puts it, "I may not be able to defeat God but I aim to worry him."

I AM THE EGG LORD
HEAR ME WHISK

(say loudly with pride)

VISIT LURPAK.CO.UK/GOODFOODFINDER

Pleasing to read? You betcha.

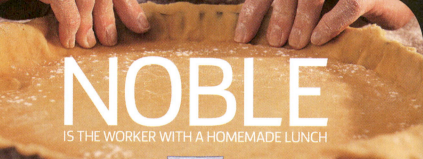

NOBLE
IS THE WORKER WITH A HOMEMADE LUNCH

GOOD FOOD DESERVES LURPAK

SALVATION
CANNOT BE FOUND IN A GARAGE PASTY

GOOD FOOD DESERVES LURPAK

Does it leave a striking image?

In many situations stickiness is an index of how rich you made your writing. Among other things, that means resisting clichés. No matter how strongly your client feels about a particular subject, we beg you to never, ever describe them as "passionate." Even if it's true, it's a worn-out word that screams "WARNING: Hack at work." And most of the time it's a dirty lie.

Is it pleasing to read?

By "pleasing" we mean does it flow, is it well written in a formal sense, is its style appropriate, and perhaps above all, *is it interesting*? Notice we don't say "entertaining"; that's fine if the topic can support it, but most can't. Instead we say "interesting" in its true sense—of interest to readers. And that comes back to the relevancy thing we talked about earlier. One thing's for sure, if the copywriter was bored writing it, then the reader will be bored reading it. Perhaps the ideal situation is when you can't help thinking or talking about the line you've just written, to the point of becoming a pest to your colleagues or partner. Sticky starts with you.

Now you have a go

We've explained the background to making a message memorable, we've introduced some techniques to help increase your interest levels, and we've outlined some ways to check your progress while writing. Now it's time for you to put all this into practice by writing us some sticky lines.

One piece of advice: don't hold back—now's the time to really let rip. Be bold and brilliant; even if you think you've gone too far, *go further*. In fact we suggest you *always* push your work as far as your imagination will allow; rest assured your client/boss will bring you back to earth if you've really overdone it.

Workout

PRODUCT AND CLIENT
You!

AUDIENCE
A prospective romantic partner.

TASK
Write one or more sticky lines that sell you to a prospective mate. This could be as obvious as a short dating-site ad, or as quirky as a tagline you append to your name. Or something else entirely.

BACKGROUND
Later in this book we make the point that pretty much everything —including individuals—can be considered a brand. This exercise is about putting Brand You into action. And hey, you might get a date out of it.

Lesson Four:
A Catalogue of Swindles and Perversions

What George Orwell can teach copywriters today

The man himself.

Lessons Two and Three work together to help you improve the art and craft of your writing. This lesson adds color to what you've just read, with priceless rules to rev up your writing from one of the true greats of twentieth-century literature.

In 1946 George Orwell—ex-private schoolboy, Spanish Civil War veteran, and one-time vagrant —published his now-famous essay, *Politics and the English Language.* Although a critique of the blather and balderdash employed by professional politicians in the 1930s and '40s, Orwell's observations are remarkably perceptive and have much to say to copywriters today.

In this lesson we'll take you through Orwell's essay, commenting on it and pointing out its relevance as we go. We strongly advise you to read the original—it's freely available on the Web, it's written in an easy, accessible style, and it's certainly worth an hour of your time. Orwell once commented that "good prose should be like a windowpane, in the sense that its meaning should be perfectly clear—a quality *Politics and the English Language* has in abundance. Give it a go.

"Good prose should be like a windowpane."

Why are we bothering you with the thoughts of a long-dead novelist? For the simple reason that Orwell was a supremely talented prose stylist. We don't mean he was a posturing virtuoso, running up and down the scales like Mozart on amphetamine, but rather that he had a profound understanding of how to make language work. The *New York Times Book Review* recently included a letter suggesting, "If you want to achieve true mastery of English prose, read Gibbon and Orwell, then shoot yourself." That may be going a little too far, but Orwell undoubtedly had a gift for getting his ideas down on paper with an inspiring blend of clarity, brevity, and impact—which is good copywriting in a nutshell. That's why Orwell matters, and that's what this lesson is about.

POLITICS AND THE ENGLISH LANGUAGE

GEORGE ORWELL

The essay itself.

Personable copy that celebrates everyday language and takes a stand against the windy waffle Orwell hated.

WE DELIVER

(We don't mean in a poncey, corporate speak kind of way, we mean in a 'we'll drop your stuff around later, for free' kind of way.)

YESTERDAY YOU SAID TOMORROW

JUST DO IT.

MY BUTT IS BIG
AND ROUND LIKE THE LETTER C
AND TEN THOUSAND LUNGES
HAVE MADE IT ROUNDER
BUT NOT SMALLER
AND THAT'S JUST FINE.
IT'S A SPACE HEATER
FOR MY SIDE OF THE BED
IT'S MY AMBASSADOR
TO THOSE WHO WALK BEHIND ME
IT'S A BORDER COLLIE
THAT HERDS SKINNY WOMEN
AWAY FROM THE BEST DEALS
AT CLOTHING SALES.
MY BUTT IS BIG
AND THAT'S JUST FINE
AND THOSE WHO MIGHT SCORN IT
ARE INVITED TO KISS IT.
JUST DO IT.

NIKEWOMEN.COM ✓

Politics and the English Language

Let's begin, appropriately enough, at the beginning. Orwell starts his essay thus:

Most people who bother with the matter at all would admit that the English language is in a bad way, but it is generally assumed that we cannot by conscious action do anything about it.

As a copywriter with a keen interest in language, Orwell's phrase "most people" includes you. Is it an exaggeration to say our language is in trouble? What do you think? Orwell's own view is pessimistic (not without reason, as the examples we'll come to in a moment make clear) but ultimately positive, in that he offers a range of practical techniques we can use to change things.

The second part of the sentence highlights the common belief that language is a given and something that can't be altered. In fact, as Orwell goes on to show, it's easily changed, and indeed it's up to all of us to alter it whenever we think it necessary. We think that's a pretty important mission.

Next Orwell offers "five specimens of the English language as it is now habitually written" that "illustrate various of the mental vices from which we now suffer" —or to put it another way, a bunch of examples that show what's wrong with contemporary writing. To give you a flavor, here's the first:

> *I am not, indeed, sure whether it is not true to say that the Milton who once seemed not unlike a seventeenth-century Shelley had not become, out of an experience ever more bitter in each year, more alien to the founder of that Jesuit sect which nothing could induce him to tolerate.*

Professor Harold Laski (*Essay in Freedom of Expression*)

Lordy. Orwell's complaint about lack of precision seems entirely justified. Remarkably, this sort of

Copy rooted in reality. According to legend, "Just do it" took just 20 minutes to write, yet still works brilliantly well 30+ years later.

convoluted writing is still common, as a quick trip to plainlanguage.gov, or plainenglish.co.uk (for UK examples), will confirm. Here's an example taken from a project Roger worked on recently. To stop your brain melting we've included a translation:

Before

Effectual winter upkeep of transport infrastructure poses sizable logistical challenges for all those responsible for maintaining the smooth running of road systems.

After

During winter it can be hard to keep roads open.

What's remarkable is that the "before" version displays the same shortcomings and "mental vices" Orwell railed against over 60 years ago. As he put it:

The writer either has a meaning and cannot express it, or he inadvertently says something else, or he is almost indifferent as to whether his words mean anything or not.

Before adding:

This mixture of vagueness and sheer incompetence is the most marked characteristic of modern English prose.

Unfortunately there's some truth in this. As the above examples show, it's not hard to find professionally written text that appears determined to avoid saying anything. Orwell goes on:

As soon as certain topics are raised, the concrete melts into the abstract and no one seems able to think of turns of speech that are not hackneyed.

We call this tone of voice "default bureaucratic"—it's what inexperienced writers reach for when they lack the confidence to express themselves in any other way (we don't say this as a criticism, simply as a fact). "Default bureaucratic" is characterized by rambling sentences, unfocused paragraphs, passive verbs, poor word choice, and—above all—no real understanding of the reader and why they're reading the piece in the

Ben Kay

The best advice I ever read about writing is this: The writer's only responsibility is to get the reader to turn the page.

That's truly brilliant because it's very easy to lose sight of the point of a piece of writing. Often a writer will try to persuade the reader of his or her genius, or cram in every possible piece of information, or worry that they're not good enough.

But none of that matters.

Whether you're P. G. Wodehouse, Jeffrey Archer, or a copywriter working on a 20x4 press ad for cut-price asparagus, if you're not getting the reader to read on then you aren't doing your job.

That task can be accomplished in many ways. Mr. Wodehouse would write such wonderful sentences and such hilarious jokes that the reader would want to extend their experience. Mr. Archer, like him or not, uses plotting, structure, and themes to keep millions of people turning the page. And the copywriter can't just stop at the asparagus's price; he must express it in a way that makes the reader want to find out where the offer is available and care enough to do something about it.

The really great thing about this rule is that it removes the spurious concept of *quality* from the process. After all, what is quality? There are a million subjective answers. For some it is about originality; for others it concerns elegance of phrase; for still others it lies in immaculate, labyrinthine plotting, but none of those things can be objectively evaluated. You can and should only do what you think is good. In fact do whatever the hell you like—just get your reader to turn the page.

At school, English was the only subject Ben was good at, but he didn't fancy doing a huge amount of work, so when he left he found a job as a copywriter at AMV BBDO in London. To his great shock he soon discovered that a great deal of work was required. From AMV he became Creative Director of Lunar BBDO, but in his spare time he wrote a novel (*Instinct*) that was published by Penguin in December 2010. Ben is now Creative Director of Media Arts Lab, working exclusively on Apple's advertising across Europe, but in his spare time he continues to write novels and screenplays.

first place. Note, "default bureaucratic"; we'll return to this textual turd several times before we're done.

Back to *Politics and the English Language*. Orwell complains that:

> *Prose consists less and less of words chosen for the sake of their meaning, and more and more of phrases tacked together like the sections of a prefabricated henhouse.*

This is a recurring nightmare for Orwell—clear, original writing supplanted by the splicing together of clichés. The result isn't writing, it's *assembling*—a patchwork of existing phrases cobbled together to fill a space.

Next Orwell describes four "tricks by means of which the work of prose construction is habitually dogged" —dying metaphors, verbal false limbs, pretentious diction, and meaningless words. Let's delve a little deeper into these excrescences, which Orwell delightfully describes as a "catalogue of swindles and perversions".

Dying metaphors

Here Orwell is complaining about worn-out metaphors and over-familiar imagery. He's comfortable with *dead* metaphors (word pictures that have lost their power through overuse) and *live* metaphors (vivid verbal images that can really help comprehension). It's *dying* metaphors—phrases that have become clichés through overuse—that drive him nuts. Orwell lists some of the worst offenders as he sees it: *ring the changes, toe the line, ride roughshod over, stand shoulder to shoulder with,* and *play into the hands of.* We could add *whole new ball game*, *at the end of the day, low-hanging fruit,* or, our personal bête noir, any use of *passionate* (in a business context).

No pretentious diction or meaningless words here.

Refreshingly direct copy.
Well, it's the thought that counts.

Verbal false limbs

This section focuses on the tendency of writers to use complex verb phrases rather than straightforward, freestanding verbs. That's not as technical as it sounds; all it means is that Orwell prefers "leads" to "play a leading role in," "serves" to "serves a purpose," and so on. Nothing to disagree with there.

He's also highly critical of passive verbs (or the passive voice, as it's sometimes called), a consistent feature of poor prose. Like Orwell we're not grammar sticklers, but active and passive verbs are something all copywriters really do need to understand. Don't panic, they're surprisingly straightforward, as we're about to explain.

Verbs come in two basic forms—active and passive. In the active form it's immediately clear who's performing the action mentioned in the sentence. Take the phrase "I heard it through the grapevine"—the very first word makes it clear who's doing the hearing. In the passive version—"The grapevine was where I heard it"—we don't find out who's doing what until far

later. While that's not the end of the world, passive verbs soon make a piece of writing feel flabby and vague.

There's one situation in which the passive form is perfect—when you want to avoid giving offense or attributing blame. If you're writing about a sensitive subject and you'd prefer to save someone's blushes, say something like, "This year's sales targets weren't met," instead of "Our sales team didn't meet their targets this year." Your author Roger remembers an incident at school when he accidently broke a fretsaw blade during a woodwork lesson. Roger approached his teacher with the words, "Sir, the blade got broken." Without looking up, the formidable old schoolmaster replied, "You mean, 'I broke it,' boy." Despite his questionable belief in the educational power of a sound thrashing, Mr. Howe's attitude to active vs. passive verbs was spot on.

Pretentious diction

Or to put it more directly, using showy words to seem big and clever. The author's aim, as Orwell puts it, is to "dress up a simple statement and give an air of scientific impartiality to biased judgements" or else "give an air of culture and elegance" where one is lacking. Neither is good.

Meaningless words

Many institutions seem curiously compelled to write utter drivel. What's worse, we accept it and actually expect no better. Usefully Orwell suggests a practical way for us to judge the clarity of a piece of writing—*count the syllables*. The more syllables, the further away a word is likely to be from the clarity and power of everyday speech. Sadly Microsoft Word's word count feature doesn't do syllables so you'll have to tot them up manually.

Orwell's point is that a writer's syllable count rises in direct proportion to his or her use of nonsensical, overblown language. He suggests the wordy version is the one most people would produce when asked to write something "official" sounding. Well, yes and no. Many writers do indeed pile on the syllables in formal situations. But in our experience even novice writers are perfectly capable of using what we might call a "default human" approach (rather than the "default bureaucratic" we talked about earlier)—they just need a little encouragement and permission to be direct.

So far so good, but wringing our hands like this is depressingly negative. What we need are practical suggestions to avoid these problems in the first place. Orwell obligingly offers up six questions he suggests every author should ask while writing:

- What am I trying to say?
- What words will express it?
- What image or idiom will make it clearer?
- Is this image fresh enough to have an effect?
- Could I put it more shortly?
- Have I said anything that is avoidably ugly?

Now we're getting to the heart of why you should bother with Orwell and his ancient essay. These questions are simple, obvious even, *but that's the point*. Good

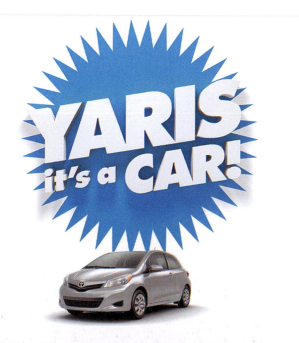

Toyota's straightforward, clear, and concise campaign for the Yaris.

copywriting isn't an arcane, mystical process; it's the result of applying simple principles with consistency.

Orwell goes as far as to say that pretty much all political writing (or in our case copywriting) is bad. On those rare occasions when this isn't the case, Orwell believes the writer must be a rebel, someone with sufficient independence of mind to express "his private opinions" and "not a party line." As he puts it, "Orthodoxy, of whatever colour, seems to demand a lifeless, imitative style." Indeed it does. In this book we encourage you to reject the lifeless conventions Orwell criticizes and embrace a vivid, accurate style that touches people's hearts and minds. You may be familiar with this:

> Here's to the crazy ones. The rebels. The troublemakers. The ones who see things differently. While some may see them as the crazy ones, we see genius. Because the people who are crazy enough to think they can change the world,
> are the ones who do.

It's the main message in TBWA\Chiat\Day's classic 1997 "Think different" campaign for Apple, and about as far from orthodox business writing as it's possible to get. As well as its rousing content, just look at the short words and tight sentences. Orwell would have approved of the ad's prose, although perhaps not its purpose.

By now you may be thinking that Orwell is dangerously close to becoming some sort of nitpicking pedant. Not so. In fact Orwell specifically states he's not interested in "correct" grammar and syntax, "which are of no importance so long as one makes one's meaning clear." Nor is he bothered about avoiding so-called Americanisms or enforcing what might be called a good prose style. He doesn't want to encourage "a fake simplicity," or the misguided belief that shorter words are always better than their longer equivalents (that's usually the case, but there are always exceptions). Orwell is simply saying we should "let the meaning choose the word, and not the other way around." This is the very heart of his argument and might be summarized as *express yourself in words that are right for your task.*

How exactly? Well, first think about what you're trying to say, and then do as Orwell suggests and "switch round and decide what impressions one's words are

To the crazy ones.

Here's to the crazy ones.
    The misfits.
      The rebels.
        The troublemakers.
          The round pegs in the square holes.
The ones who see things differently.

They're not fond of rules.
    And they have no respect for the status quo.

You can praise them, disagree with them, quote them,
    disbelieve them, glorify them or vilify them.
About the only thing you can't do is ignore them.

Because they change things.
    They invent.   They imagine.   They heal.
    They explore.   They create.   They inspire.
They push the human race forward.

Maybe they have to be crazy.
How else can you stare at an empty canvas and see a work of art?
    Or sit in silence and hear a song that's never been written?
Or gaze at a red planet and see a laboratory on wheels?

We make tools for these kinds of people.
While some see them as the crazy ones, we see genius.

Because the people who are crazy enough to think they can change the world, are the ones who do.

        Think different.

Apple's classic "Think different" ad, created by TBWA\Chiat\Day in 1997. By the end we practically want to leap up and shout, "Yes, YES! THAT'S ME! I'm CRAZY and PROUD! Where do I sign?"

The world's longest banner ad. Gleefully ignoring Orwell's advice to cut out every unnecessary word helps this playful ad for BMW draw attention to itself.

likely to make on another person." That last part is crucial for copywriters. We write exclusively to make an impression on others, and here Orwell is telling us how to do it. As he puts it, "This last effort of the mind cuts out all stale or mixed images, all prefabricated phrases, needless repetitions, and humbug and vagueness generally."

To help us he provides his famous six rules (a sort of counterpoint to the six questions suggested earlier), the most quoted and reproduced part of his essay. Here they are:

- Never use a metaphor, simile, or other figure of speech which you are used to seeing in print.
- Never use a long word where a short one will do.
- If it is possible to cut a word out, always cut it out.
- Never use the passive where you can use the active.
- Never use a foreign phrase, a scientific word, or a jargon word if you can think of an everyday English equivalent.
- Break any of these rules sooner than say anything outright barbarous.

There's nothing magical about these. Orwell acknowledges that it's perfectly possible to write bad English using them, but not the sort of bad English we've described here with its windy vagueness, shoddy imagery, and lack of meaning.

In the final paragraph of his essay Orwell states:

If you simplify your English, you are freed from the worst follies of orthodoxy. You cannot speak any of the necessary dialects, and when you make a stupid remark its stupidity will be obvious, even to yourself.

In other words, keep it simple and any shortcomings in your work will be obvious. The result will send the "verbal refuse" of so much writing "into the dustbin, where it belongs." Amen to that.

Orwell's English in 30 seconds

Ask yourself these six questions:

- What am I trying to say?
- What words will express it?
- What image or idiom will make it clearer?
- Is this image fresh enough to have an effect?
- Could I put it more shortly?
- Have I said anything that is avoidably ugly?

Follow these six rules:

- Never use a metaphor, simile, or other figure of speech which you are used to seeing in print.
- Never use a long word where a short one will do.
- If it is possible to cut a word out, always cut it out.
- Never use the passive where you can use the active.
- Never use a foreign phrase, a scientific word, or a jargon word if you can think of an everyday English equivalent.
- Break any of these rules sooner than say anything outright barbarous.

Now you have a go

Orwell's six questions and six rules are solid gold, *but only if you actually put them to use*. Reading them through, nodding approvingly, and then forgetting about them as the pub beckons isn't exactly the path to enlightenment. To help embed Orwell's ideas in your brain we've come up with a couple of exercises we think are worthy of your attention.

Workout One

A prospective employer wants you to write a few paragraphs explaining why they should invite you for an interview.

First write your reply as you would normally (don't overthink it—just do what comes naturally). Once you're finished, rewrite it using Orwell's six questions and six rules to ruthlessly assess and improve every word and sentence. Which version is better? Why?

Workout Two

Find a speech or other piece of public writing that seems stuffed with pretentious diction, meaningless words, cloudy vagueness, and so on (any halfway decent library will have plenty of anthologies of speeches by the great and good, as does the Web).

Go through your chosen speech (or a section if it's too long) and tease out the real meaning as a list of bullet points. Next use Orwell's six questions and six rules to rewrite it so the text is clear and sparkling "like a windowpane."

Lesson Five:
It's All About the Audience

Don't solve the client's problem, solve the customer's

Prepare for an unpalatable truth: It's not about what you want to say; it's about what they—your audience—want to hear. Yes, you've got to cover the points your client briefed you on, but if that's all you do then there's a fair chance you won't really engage your audience. And that, gentle reader, is what this whole copywriting business is all about.

Clearly a man in tune with his audience.

The genuine London road sign on the right is an escapee. If you were to spend a day with your local public works department—the people responsible for road signs and the like—you'd probably hear many similar phrases bandied about. That's not surprising, as all professions develop verbal shorthands to help them do their job.[1] The problem comes when this internal language manages to sneak into the outside world. The background knowledge that made the shorthand an asset to the group isn't there to support it, leading to misunderstanding and mirth. That's what's happened here. The sign's audience has changed but its language hasn't, and our bewilderment is the result.

This principle—that language must be right for its readers—is the cornerstone of this chapter. Never just assume, as the writers of this sign clearly did, that your readers will automatically see things your way and read a message as you intend it to be read. There's every chance they won't. Instead you need to be sensitive to cultural and contextual differences. As Jeremy Bullmore, ex-JWT executive and one of the wisest men in advertising, has put it:

"Much good advertising speaks quite deliberately in code, or uses a secret language, and excludes the rest of us. That's one of the reasons why it's good."

And more evocatively:

"As the global gospelers begin to sound ever less persuasive, it is coded tribal messages we should increasingly look at with respect."

In short, messages written in the private language of a particular group can work wonders, *but only if they reach the right audience.* There's nothing necessarily wrong with the language of the above road sign, but there's everything wrong with the context in which it's used. It makes no concession to its readers and is all but incomprehensible as a result.

The "Hip Cops" poster on the facing page shows the very opposite problem—the authors have desperately tried to adopt the language of their audience but have bombed in spectacular fashion. It's a genuine recruitment poster for the Berkeley Police Department in San Francisco, created in 1969—the height of the hippie era, when peace, love, and patchouli were the order of the day:

You can almost hear the irate Chief of Police banging the table and demanding his recruitment department get more of those damn hippies to join the Force. Off goes a hapless underling and puts together this rich brew of late sixties clichés in a desperate but doomed attempt to recruit the sort of people who wouldn't work

1. What we're talking about here is jargon, and the big thing to know about jargon is it isn't necessarily bad. Jargon evolves to meet the specific communication needs of a specific group, and as long as it's used in the right circumstances it's a very effective way of communicating. In fact if you're writing for a particular group you must use their language if you want your words to have credibility. The problem, as we say, is when jargon is used in the wrong situations. That way madness lies.

WANTED

HIP COPS

We know it's a heavy trip, but there are more than 30 vacancies on the Berkeley Police force. If hip people do not apply and go on to fill those vacancies, we'll get more of the same old stuff and have the same old hassles! Put yourself on the line—and get some change for it, too. **Starting pay for Berkeley officers is $782 per month.**

We want PEACEmen, not POLICEmen

If you are sane;

If you love children and other growing things;

If you do not like the use of force when gentleness will work;

If you will defend justice for all, regardless of race, appearance or politics;

If you believe that all people should be free to live their own lives if they do not harm others;

If you value people for themselves, not for their money or dress—

THEN WE NEED YOU TO REMOLD "THE MAN" AND HIS JOB.

MINIMUM REQUIREMENTS—Applicants must:

1. Be between 20 and 29 years old.
2. Have completed two years of college.
3. Be 5'-8" or taller and of proportionate weight.
4. Have a valid driver's license.
5. Be in good health and physical condition.
6. Have at least 20/70 correctable or 20/30 eyesight.

You must also be willing to undergo a medical examination, take a loyalty oath, and have a background check. You must be a United States citizen but need not live in Berkeley.

TO MAKE APPLICATION—Write to: Berkeley Police Department, Personnel Dept., 2100 Grove Street, Berkeley
Call: 841-0200
Recruiting information is available free from the Berkeley Police Department.

IF YOU APPLY—If you are hip (black, white, red, yellow or brown) and decide to apply, please notify the BBC or the Berkeley branch of the ACLU. We want to be sure that you are hired without prejudice as to your appearance, race, or background. BBC Patrol can be reached at 526-6370. ACLU can be reached at 548-0921, or at 1919 Berkeley Way.

Published as a public service by The Better Berkeley Council, 1534 Grove Street, Berkeley

ATTENTION HIPSTER DOOFUSES:

SORRY ABOUT THAT, BUT IT'S NOT EASY GETTING THE ATTENTION OF PEOPLE WHO REJECT MAINSTREAM CONSUMERISM LIKE BILLIONAIRES REJECT TAX OVERHAUL. HERE'S THE THING: DO YOU EVER WAKE UP IN YOUR DESIGNER PLATFORM BED IN YOUR URBAN LOFT, SHUFFLE OVER TO YOUR ESPRESSO MACHINE AND WONDER: IS THIS ALL THERE IS? DAY AFTER DAY OF WEARING IRONIC VINTAGE TEE SHIRTS AND SEARCHING THE INTERNET FOR NU RAVE TECHNO RAP BANDS FROM UZBEKISTAN? DON'T YOU WISH YOU COULD LET YOUR ANDROGYNOUSLY CUT HAIR DOWN, WEAR SOME NOT-QUITE-SO-PAINFULLY-SKINNY JEANS AND KICK BACK AND WATCH THE (LEGAL IN ALL 50 STATES VERSION OF) GRASS GROW? NOT TO GET ALL MARKETINGY, BUT AT URBAN EATERY YOU CAN TAKE A BREAK FROM LOOKING VAGUELY DISINTERESTED IN EVERYTHING WHILE WEARING YOUR FAVORITE ORGANIC FEDORA. WE USE FRESH INGREDIENTS FROM LOCAL FARMS AND OFFER FREE VALET PARKING— AND FREE IS NICE IF YOU HAVE ONE OF THOSE HIPSTER LIBERAL ARTS DEGREES. SO WHY NOT TAKE SOME TIME OUT OF YOUR BUSY SCHEDULE OF WRESTLING WITH EXISTENTIAL ANGST AND DROP BY URBAN EATERY. AFTER A HARD WEEK OF CONFORMING TO NONCONFORMITY, YOU'VE EARNED IT.

URBAN **EATERY**
— FREE VALET PARKING —

Copy that gently mocks its audience, yet
somehow ends up celebrating the very
thing it ridicules.

for The Man in a million years. They've tried to speak the language of their intended readership, but in doing so they've stumbled into a great, yawning authenticity gap. Like a broken bell it doesn't ring true.

The point we're making with these two examples is that *audiences are everything when it comes to crafting an effective message*. In fact the main reason any piece of copy doesn't work is that the writer has failed to consider their reader. What this means is that when you're planning a piece you need to start at the *end* of the communications process, with the people who will read your words. Any other perspective is asking for trouble.

In the coming pages we'll explore this idea in more detail. To make matters simple we've structured what follows in an intuitive way—if copywriting is about *audiences*, then audiences are about **content**, **expression**, **identity**, and **self-interest**.

Audiences are about content

What exactly do you want to achieve?

"It's only words,
And words are all I have,
to take your heart away."

"Words" by the Bee Gees

How right Barry, Robin, and Maurice Gibb were—like the lovelorn suitor in their 1968 ballad, words are the only thing we copywriters have to create meaning and achieve results. This highlights the intimate connection between content (what we say) and purpose (what we're trying to achieve). If what we write misses the

mark with our readers then whatever result we were hoping for will be compromised. If that happens, all the eloquence, fine design, and technical trickery in the world won't make any difference—the audience will notice its irrelevancy and treat it accordingly.

So when thinking about content we need to match our message to our readers' lives. In fact you could define copywriting as communication written with the reader in mind. Poets, playwrights, and novelists write for themselves; copywriters write for others. Make no mistake, ours is an audience-driven occupation.

Creating reader-friendly content

Start by thinking about your reader's state of mind. If it's ignorance, your mission is to inform. If it's opposition, you need to create agreement. If it's indifference, you need to generate interest. If possible, it's worth briefly discussing their problem/issue in your copy—it shows you understand where they're coming from. And of course, the more significant the problem you describe, the more a reader will appreciate your solution.

Above all, you need to *solve the customer's problem, not the client's.* Chances are they're not the same thing. The client will have a particular marketing issue they wish to address; the customer couldn't care less. Instead you need to bring the benefit to life—to *their life.* Start from where your readers are at and you'll get through to them. Ignore them and you're done for.

I WANT TO MAKE A HORROR MOVIE

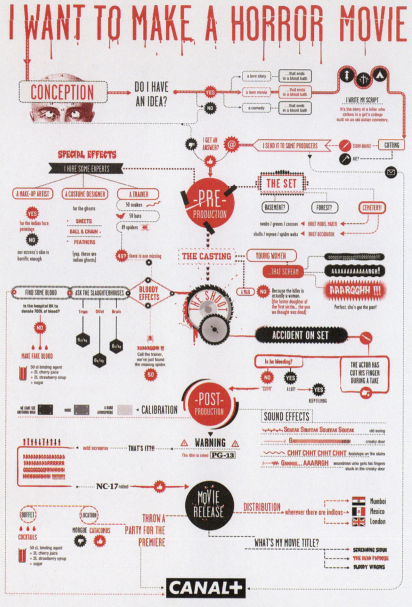

CONCEPTION

DO I HAVE AN IDEA?

YES
- a love story ...that ends in a blood bath
- a teen movie ...that ends in a blood bath
- a comedy ...that ends in a blood bath

NO

I WRITE MY SCRIPT
It's the story of a killer who strikes in a girl's college built on an old indian cemetery.

I GET AN ANSWER?   @   I SEND IT TO SOME PRODUCERS   STORY-BOARD?   CUTTING

AXE?

SPECIAL EFFECTS

I HIRE SOME EXPERTS

-PRE- PRODUCTION

THE SET
- BASEMENT?
- FOREST?
- CEMETERY!

tombs / graves / crosses   BRIEF MODEL MAKER
skulls / tepees / spider webs   BRIEF DECORATOR

A MAKE-UP ARTIST
YES for the indian face paintings
NO our actress's skin is horrific enough

A COSTUME DESIGNER
for the ghosts
- SHEETS
- BALL & CHAIN
- FEATHERS
(yep, these are indian ghosts)

A TRAINER
50 snakes
50 bats
49 spiders
49? there is one missing

THE CASTING

YOUNG WOMEN
...THAT SCREAM
AAAAAAAAAAARGH!
aaaaaaaarrrggaaashhhhhhhhhhhh!!!

A MAN   NO   Because the killer is actually a woman, (the former daughter of the first victim... the one we thought was dead)
AAARGGHH !!!
Perfect, she's got the part!

FIND SOME BLOOD
Is the hospital OK to donate 700L of blood?
NO
MAKE FAKE BLOOD
50 cl binding agent + 2L cherry juice + 2L strawberry sirup + sugar

ASK THE SLAUGHTERHOUSES
Tripe   Offal   Brain
5L/kg   6L/kg   8L/kg

BLOODY EFFECTS

AAARGGHH !!!
Call the trainer, we've just found the missing spider.
50

THE SHOOT

ACCIDENT ON SET

Is he bleeding?
NO "CUT?!"   YES A LOT?   YES KEEP FILMING

THE ACTOR HAS CUT HIS FINGER DURING A TAKE

-POST- PRODUCTION

CALIBRATION
WE CAN'T SEE ANYTHING NOW   MORE   A DARK ATMOSPHERE

SOUND EFFECTS
- Squeak Squeak Squeak Squeak   old swing
- Giiiiiiiiiiiiiiiii   creaky door
- CHHT CHHT CHHT CHHT   footsteps on the stairs
- Giiiiiii.... AAARRGH   soundman who gets his fingers stuck in the creaky door

add screams   THAT'S IT?!!   ⚠ WARNING ⚠
The film is rated PG-13

AAAAAAAAAAAAAAAAAAA
AAAAAAAAARRRRRR
OOOOOOOOGGGHHHHHHH
HHHHHHHHH !!!!!!!!

NC-17 rated

MOVIE RELEASE

DISTRIBUTION   wherever there are indians
- Mumbai
- Mexico
- London

WHAT'S MY MOVIE TITLE?
- SCREAMING SIOUX
- THE DEAD PAPOOSE
- BLOODY VIRGINS

BUFFET
COCKTAILS
50 cL binding agent + 2L cherry juice + 2L strawberry sirup + sugar

LOCATION
MORGUE   CATACOMBS

THROW A PARTY FOR THE PREMIERE

CANAL+

SHOOTING A FILM ISN'T THAT SIMPLE
CANAL+ SUPPORTS THOSE WHO MAKE MOVIES

The aim here is to show Canal+'s understanding of movie making. Given that their audience includes a healthy percentage of wannabe movie makers, it's saying "Hey, we're all the same here."

Headlines for our times. There's nothing like tapping into the zeitgeist to create a bit of reader appeal.

Audiences are about expression

Whose voice should we hear when we read the words?

Expression—in this context—means tone of voice. Those three little words have generated much interest and analysis in recent years. Indeed, "tone of voice" is the one phrase that more or less everyone in marketing, design, branding, and advertising knows about copywriting, so the chances are you'll hear it bandied about with enthusiasm, if not precision.

For us, tone of voice is *the combination of what you say and how you say it*. We looked at *what you say* in the previous section; here we focus on *how you say it*. We've thought about this long and hard, and come to the conclusion that the best way to understand tone of voice is to ask, "Whose voice should we hear in our head as we read the words?"

Think of your favorite novelist or screenwriter—one of the things that makes them good is their ability to create convincing, compelling voices for their characters. It's the same for you. If you can create a voice for your copy with some of the same qualities, then you'll bring your work to life.

A quick example

Your mission is to create some copy for a brochure selling high-power surf kites. The brief says that the tone of voice should be "compelling, energetic, irreverent, and exciting," which seems fair enough given the subject and intended readership. What do these adjectives mean in practice? "Compelling" might mean including plenty of persuasive facts, "energetic" might mean short sentences and a staccato paragraph structure, as well as lots of emotive trigger words. "Irreverent" could translate into a bit of humor and permission not to take anything too seriously, and "exciting" demands you convey the undoubted thrill of

Wendy Ide

By the time you read this it will already be out of date. Print journalism (and my small corner of it, film criticism) is evolving at such a rate that who knows what wrench will have been chucked into the machinery in six months' time? With that in mind, is there any advice I can give to people starting out in an industry that bears little or no resemblance to the one I broke into? Well, yes. One or two things remain the same.

1. Never, ever miss a deadline.

2. Be polite to the subeditors. They have a thankless job and they have the power to make you look better or worse than you are. Making enemies of the subs is on a par to insulting someone who has the opportunity to spit in your food.

3. Be versatile. Learn every skill you can, specifically anything to do with digital publishing.

4. Blog your ass off. Tweet well and tweet often. For editors groping in the dark to find the future of publishing, an online presence is something they respect (even if they might not fully understand it or its uses).

Before Wendy joined *The Times* as a film critic and features writer in 2004 she had worked extensively for publications such as *Dazed & Confused*, *Sight & Sound*, *Elle*, and the *Sunday Herald*. She has been writing about—and working within—the film industry since 1996. She's been a programmer for the London Film Festival, patron of the London Children's Film Festival, and jury member for film festivals in San Sebastian, the Czech Republic, the UK, and Zanzibar.

surf-kite action. Put it all together and the opening spread might read something like this:

The Raptor Series

Respect is due

Raptor isn't for holiday flyers; it's aimed at experienced adrenaline junkies who take a perverse pleasure in pushing themselves to the limit.

These kites are potent—so potent it's essential you understand what you're getting into. The only way to appreciate the sheer arm-wrenching, gut-churning, butt-clenching pull of a Raptor kite's 300lb of lift is to fly one. Take it too far and Raptor will beat you every time.

Like we say, respect is due.

OK, we could have written that a hundred other ways, but the above does the job and certainly matches the tone-of-voice adjectives supplied.

So to summarize, tone of voice is the combination of what you say and how you say it. The result is a brand's personality in print (or indeed pixels). The reason tone matters is because different audiences respond to different tones—the above example with its "arm-wrenching" hyperbole is very male; copy aimed at female kiters would require less obvious machismo while still retaining the same sense of excitement—a rather trickier writing challenge. And on that point, let's look at audiences and identity.

Audiences are about identity

Are you talking to me?

"Who's my audience?" is perhaps the most important question a copywriter can ask. The brief—assuming you've got one—may be some help, outlining your potential readership in terms like, "Aspirational single male, 25–35, with above-average income and strong interest in intimate waxing." It's a start, but it's too broad and generic.

You need the clearest possible picture of your reader, which means zooming in from the general to the specific. Who exactly are these wealthy, waxing-obsessed men? What's their story? How do they speak? What would make them listen? As the copywriter you need to know. Do you know anyone similar you could use as a model? If so, they're your target—picture them as you write and reject anything that feels off-target.

Above all, think of your audience as individuals with whom you're having a one-to-one conversation. As copywriter Alastair Crompton puts it, "Never try to speak to everyone; you'll end up reaching no one."

David Ogilvy felt much the same:

"I don't write to the crowd. I try to write from one human being to another human being using the second person singular."

To get through to your reader you need to know who they are and what they care about. And it's to the unfortunately named topic of *care abouts* that we now turn.

2. The writer of these ads—Matt Porter of M&C Saatchi in Sydney, Australia—told us, "A tip I've never forgotten is to visualize somebody I know who epitomizes the audience and write my copy as if it was a letter to them. So if I were writing for a product my mother would be keen on, I'd start with 'Dear Mom,' and remove it at the end. It just allows me to write in a way that doesn't sound like a salesman. Here I had to address my audience's perception of polo as an elitist activity. To convince the average Aussie to take a second look at a sport they'd never considered watching we had to demonstrate that polo could poke fun at itself. So we tackled the problem head-on with the most ostentatious headlines imaginable. The audience saw this as an invitation. After all, in Australia if you can take the piss out of yourself, you're a good bloke. Once the first headline was written, the others came quite quickly—I just took dictation basically."

Something rather clever is going on here. The copy speaks directly to a nonexistent audience of imagined playboy types, and in doing so it asks the real audience to identify with this lofty group just for a moment. Given that the advertiser's mission was to popularize the usually exclusive sport of polo it's a witty, effective approach.[2]

If you thought it was hard leaving home at 18, try doing it at 72.

If the first time you left home it seemed exciting, fresh and a little bit scary, the last time you leave it might just be plain scary. But if you're struggling to cope with the stairs it may be a step you're considering. Why not give one of our experienced advisors a call on 0800 715 140 and we'll tell you everything you need to know about stairlifts and staying in the home you love.

Call 0800 715 140 ext. 5519

www.stannahstairlifts.co.uk

Stannah
The Stairlift People

Empathy is everything

The key word here is empathy—the ability to feel what the reader feels, to identify with them, to put yourself in their shoes. It's said that one of the reasons Avis Car Rental's classic "We try harder" campaign worked so well was that its target audience—salesmen who needed to rent a car—could easily identify with the idea of struggling against a dominant competitor. They knew what it was like to be number two and to try harder. The copy understood the people it was talking to—in short, it empathized.

The question, of course, is how to do this. The answer is to ask yourself, "If I were the reader, what would *I* want to know? What would make *me* read the next line? And the next?" And so on. The better you can do this, the better the connection you'll make. Needless to say, your identification with the reader needs to sound natural, spontaneous, and appropriate. Get this right and the result will stand out a mile.

We're indebted to writers John Simmons and Jamie Jauncey for the next example of "put yourself in their shoes" writing: the annual letter from über investor Warren Buffett to the shareholders of his business, Berkshire Hathaway. These letters demonstrate Mr. Buffett's magisterial command of his subject and his remarkable ability to get inside his readers' heads. The former isn't too surprising for the world's top financial wizard but the latter certainly is—until you learn that Buffett always writes as though he's talking to his sisters, Doris and Bertie. The result is charming and informative in equal measure. Here's the opening of his 2010 letter:

> *The highlight of 2010 was our acquisition of Burlington Northern Santa Fe, a purchase that's working out even better than I expected. It now appears that owning this railroad will increase Berkshire's "normal" earning power by nearly 40% pre-tax and by well over 30% after-tax. Making this*

Copy written from the audience's point of view that empathizes with their concerns. Note the nonpatronizing tone—friendly, informal, and understanding without any cloying sentimentality.

The I'VE JUST SPLIT UP Collection

We know how it feels. You don't even want to wake up in the morning. Your confidence has taken a bit of a knock and we understand. So much so we've prepared a little Collection to cheer you up. Especially, since you have a little more time on your hands now. (Sorry). Ready to feel better? First, stand in front of the Pre-Raphaelite masterpiece 'Ophelia' from Hamlet by Millais. See? Someone else went through that too. Her loneliness should make you feel… less lonely, strangely enough. Maybe it's not the end of the world for you. Actually, you should look at the monumental 'The Last Judgement' by John Martin in Room 9. Now, that is the end of the world, quite literally. This painting will help you put things in perspective, so no more sobbing, alright? Now we should talk about your future. Think about it, you're facing a moment of endless possibilities, a bit like Simon Patterson's contemporary work 'The Great Bear' in Room 26. (You know, the one with the underground map.) It means that anything can happen. So comb your hair because you never know who's around. Now, you're ready for a Turner Stand in front of 'Sunrise, with a Boat between Headlands.' Its highlights represent the idea of a bright new beginning. Everything will be okay. And remember, we're always here for you (10.00 – 17.50 daily).

Create your own Collection

Admission Free   Pimlico
www.tate.org.uk   Millbank Pier

British Art Displays 1500 – 2006
Supported by BP

BRITAIN
TATE

This ad for Tate Britain shows a real understanding of who goes to galleries these days and why. The text puts itself well and truly in its readers' shoes.

The **I'M HUNGOVER** Collection

OK. Right now you're in a very particular emotional state. We understand, so we've put together a mini Collection for you with lots of stops for a sit down. Firstly, we need to run a check on you. Are we talking about a 'Cholmondeley Ladies' hangover or a 'Heads of Six of Hogarth's Servants' hangover? A 'Cholmondeley Ladies' hangover is fine as it is a portrait of identical twins and means you are just seeing double. The other is slightly more serious as Hogarth painted six portraits swirling around on a single canvas, and if this is what your head feels like then you're in trouble. If you are feeling some guilt, a visit to the Vatican might help redeem your soul. Have a look at Richard Wilson's picture of the Vatican in Room 6, showing a splendid morning view from a hill above the Tiber. (Stand still until you see just one Vatican). Now, let's ease your headache. What you need is a strong dose of the 'The Plains of Heaven' by John Martin in Room X. This hypnotizing image oozes tranquillity and harmony, whilst the blissful landscape represents salvation. You should be feeling better now. Just to make sure that the symptoms are completely gone, we need to run another quick check. The painting of 'The Cock Tavern' in Room 7 is a good test as it portrays a classic English country pub. If you can bear to stare at it for a decent amount. of time, it means you're cured. Don't get any ideas about going out again though; it's an eight o'clock bedtime for you tonight.

Create your own Collection

Admission Free   ⊖ Pimlico
www.tate.org.uk   🚢 Millbank Pier

British Art Displays 1500 – 2006
Supported by BP

BRITAIN
TATE

Never jog alone again. Or more realistically, never watch TV alone again.

 adopt a new life.
THS TORONTO HUMANE SOCIETY.com

I am an excellent source of outside.

adopt a new life.
THS TORONTO HUMANE SOCIETY.com

Charming copy for the Toronto Humane Society that focuses on the real reasons and benefits of owning a dog.

purchase increased our share count by 6% and used $22 billion of cash. Since we've quickly replenished the cash, the economics of this transaction have turned out very well.

We particularly love the first-person perspective. Contrast that with the exact equivalent from mega-bank Goldman Sachs:

2010 was a period of strong performance for Goldman Sachs in the context of a challenging year. We contended with uncertainty about the outlook for the global economy, questions about the future of regulation and significant scrutiny of our industry and Goldman Sachs. Despite these considerable challenges, our results were driven by two related and critical factors: (1) our clients, who turned to Goldman Sachs for advice and execution across a broad set of global businesses and (2) the focused commitment and dedication of our people to serving our clients' needs and to strengthening our culture of teamwork and excellence.

Perhaps a certain type of reader appreciates such off-the-shelf phrases as "challenging year," "contended with uncertainty," and "our culture of teamwork and excellence."[3] Perhaps, but we doubt it. There's no empathy—it's all "us" and no "you." If there's one thing guaranteed to catch an audience's attention it's something that relates directly to them, as we're about to find out.

Audiences are about self-interest

What do your readers really want to know?

We humans are all motivated—to one extent or another—by self-interest. Not necessarily the grasping, nasty kind; more a softer, gentler sort of selfishness that quietly asks, "What's in it for me?"

For copywriters this means explaining the *benefit* of whatever we're writing about, not the features. You may need to cover the latter in order to properly express the former, but your emphasis must always be on the audience payoff. Many wise and venerable sayings have emerged in the world of advertising that make this very point, from Elmer Wheeler's "Sell the sizzle, not the steak," to John Caples's advice about emphasizing "the world's best lawn" and not "the world's best lawn seed." Direct-mail expert Victor Schwab even went as far as composing a brief ditty on this very subject that ends:

So tell me quick and tell me true/ (Or else, my love, to hell with you!)/ Less—how this product came to be/ More—what the damn thing does for me!

Schwab was highlighting the fact that many organizations think of their own agenda instead of asking themselves, "What can we do to make people want to read what we have to say?" In practice this often means forcing their copywriters to shoehorn in far too much information. A better approach for all concerned would be to concentrate on one or two things that really ignite the audience's imagination and leave the rest for elsewhere.

It's a myth that readers want to know everything right away. They don't. What they want to know is, er, what they want to know. Far from being unhelpful, this tautology is a key principle of effective copywriting —if the writer can somehow find out what really

3. Orwell's splicing together of clichés, anyone?

excites their reader, then delivering that in the right way becomes infinitely easier. As so often with creative work, to accurately define the problem is halfway to finding a solution.

What does this mean in practical writing terms? Simply that you find your strongest theme—almost certainly focusing on benefits—and stick to it. Relatively few sales are made purely on a piece of copy (in the sense someone reads our words and immediately whips out their credit card). Instead our work tends to be part of a larger convincing process, with the actual deal being sealed elsewhere. Nine times out of ten our aim is to get people to take the next step—nothing more. We need to focus on that and ignore all distractions.

To test how well you're doing, once you've got something halfway decent down on paper you should pause and ask yourself how its intended audience would read it. Is it complete? Is the tone right? Does it explain itself? Will readers warm to it? What assumptions does it make? Are these assumptions reasonable, given what you know about the reader? Then correct any shortcomings before asking the same questions. Continue this way until your writing matches what readers want to read. It's a question of flipping between being a writer and a reader and a writer and…well, you get the idea.

Now you have a go

Throughout this chapter we've emphasized that good copywriting talks its readers' language. But don't take our word for it—instead we want you to explore the idea of tone of voice, content, audience, and context in these two exercises.

Workout One

Find two brands with a clear, easily identifiable tone of voice. Ideally these brands should appeal to very different audiences—one might be consumer-focused and the other public service or trade-orientated. Describe these two tones of voice using four or five appropriate adjectives each.

Now take a chunk of copy associated with Brand A (ideally the bit you used to find the adjectives describing A's tone of voice—perhaps their homepage text) and rewrite it using the adjectives for Brand B. Repeat the process the other way round—use Brand B's adjectives to rewrite Brand A's content.

Do the results work? If not, why not? Is there any way you could make the remix successful? Does content override tone of voice, or vice versa? How do you think the two brand's audiences would react to the remixed text?

Workout Two

We've said good copywriting always remembers its readers and is sensitive to its context. Let's see if that's true.

Write a straightforward text ad (headline and optional body copy) for sanitary towels to run in a lads' magazine called *Bikes, Birds, and Booze*. Now do the same for a new penis enlargement product that will appear on a feminist website called www.radikavlsisterz.com.

You don't get paid if the ads don't run, so avoid causing unnecessary offense. Instead find a way to present these products in ways that somehow appeal to their unusual new audiences.

Lesson Six:
Not Telling Stories, Selling Stories

The power of narrative to convince by stealth

The storytelling party, from *Alice's Adventures in Wonderland* by Lewis Carroll.

In her 1968 poem "The Speed of Darkness," the poet Muriel Rukeyser wrote, "The universe is made of stories, not of atoms." It's a lovely image, suggesting life is the sum of the tales we tell. It's also pretty accurate—we're hardwired to rework events into a coherent narrative as we attempt to understand the world. So come with us as we explore how stories can help copywriters communicate with power and personality. Are you sitting comfortably? Then we'll begin...

The Globe Theatre, Southwark, London, 1599, about teatime. A group of players assemble on stage, among them William Shakespeare, the chap responsible for tonight's entertainment. Instinctively the groundlings quieten down and the fruitsellers mute their cries. As hush descends, the scene begins:

Now is the winter of our reduced sales forecast, Seasonally adjusted to reflect adverse trading conditions.

An apple core hits Richard III right between the eyes —shot! Another causes the Duke of Clarence to dodge, knocking the ghost of King Henry VI to the ground in a clatter of stage armor. The crowd roars in delight and the attack intensifies, their displeasure all too apparent. This isn't what they paid to see...

Needless to say, this surreal scene never happened. Then, as now, what theatergoers want—what we all want—are stories, because stories are an important part of what it is to be human.[1] If you're trying to get through to people, the cant and cliché of business-speak is the biggest turn-off imaginable. You won't be pelted with rotten fruit but you *will* be ignored—which in our line of work is just as bad.

From a copywriting perspective stories matter because they're fun and functional at the same time. Fun because they're naturally appealing and we're primed from birth to accept information presented in narrative form; functional because they're powerful explaining tools that enable us to describe the who, what, where, when, why, and how of a subject without seeming to. That's why stories are important and that's why every copywriter needs to know when and how to switch into storytelling mode.

The scene.

1. In his book *The Storytelling Animal*, Jonathan Gottschall suggests this is because we use story as a sort of mental flight simulator, enabling us to try out situations, characters, emotions, and outcomes without all the dangers and difficulties associated with doing the same in real life.

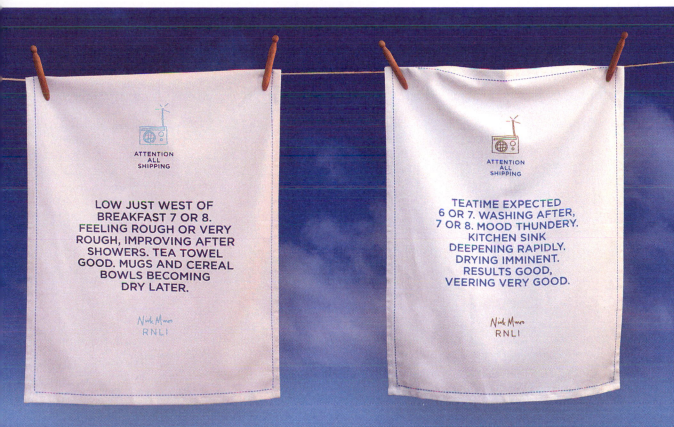

"Attention all shipping" are the first words of BBC Radio's Shipping Forecast, a weather bulletin covering the seas around the British Isles. Over the decades the Shipping Forecast has become famous for its measured pace, hypnotic delivery, and evocative place names ("Shannon, Rockall, Malin, west 8, occasionally 9, becoming cyclonic later..."). These microstories—written by Roger—twist the Shipping Forecast's distinctive language to suit a series of domestic situations vaguely connected to various items of homeware—appropriate enough, given the client is the Royal National Lifeboat Institution, the charity that runs the UK and Ireland's lifeboat service.

What exactly do we mean by "stories"?

In this context "story" refers to anything from a short anecdote to a lengthy tale. It probably doesn't begin "Once upon a time," although brand stories (as we'll call them) often include features we associate with literary stories. For example, many brand stories feature some sort of hero who struggles with some sort of antihero, leading to resolution and a happy ending where everyone goes home wiser. What matters is the effect, not the word count or format. For us, brand stories are about creating engagement. The good news is that shouldn't be too hard to achieve, as stories are engagement machines *par excellence*.

Like any good story, a brand story should be clear, compelling, and built around a strong central idea. If it isn't clear then no one will learn anything meaningful, if it isn't compelling then readers will drift off halfway through and start thinking about lunch, and if it isn't built around a powerful main theme then your audience will be left wondering what point you're trying to make.

Another important feature is struggle or difference. Aristotle suggested that, "The essence of drama is conflict." It's exactly the same here—if a brand story contains even a whiff of tension it'll become more readable and memorable as a result. It also needs to feel grounded in reality—if a brand story couldn't possibly be true then it's fantasy, not copy. The trick is to use a story vivid enough to embed itself in the readers' imagination, yet real enough to touch on or illuminate some relevant truth.

Of course stories like this demand the right sort of language; they need to use human words and focus on human themes. That's the way to establish an emotional connection with your audience, and emotional beats rational every time. Here "story" is almost a synonym for "brand," as the next section explains.

This pastiche playbill for the University of Lincoln Creative Advertising degree end-of-year show uses multiple ministries to enthrall and entertain.

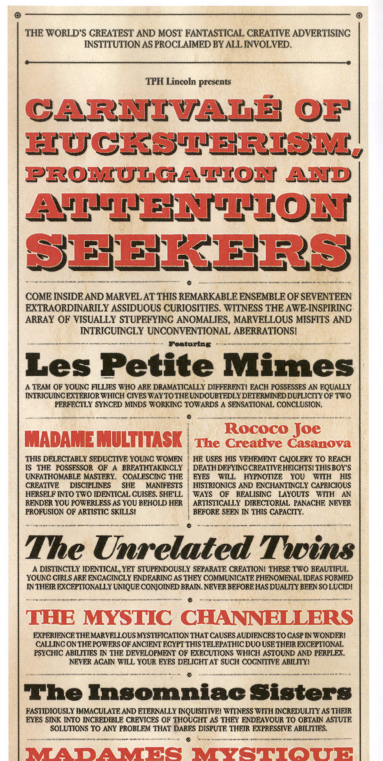

Stories as creation myths

Brand stories are a particularly effective way of explaining an organization's origins. Consider this example from hyper-successful UK smoothie-maker Innocent. It comes from their company rule book:

In the summer of 1998 when we had developed our first smoothie recipes but were still nervous about giving up our proper jobs, we brought £500 worth of fruit, turned it into smoothies and sold them from a stall at a little music festival in London. We put up a big sign saying "Do you think we should give up our jobs to make these smoothies?" and put out a bin saying "YES" and a bin saying "NO" and asked people to put the empty bottle in the right bin.
At the end of the weekend the "YES" bin was full so we went in the next day and resigned.

It's a modern-day creation myth—only it happens to be true. Don't you feel instant affection for Innocent's fruit-loving founders? In 110 words they manage to explain when and how it all began, tell us something about their attitude to life and business, locate themselves culturally, and give us a glimpse into their organization's soul, a notoriously intangible subject that often defies direct description.

Then there's the story of how Nike cofounder Bill Bowerman poured liquid latex onto his wife's waffle iron to create a grippy sole for a new sneaker he was developing at home. That sounds suspiciously fabricated until we learn that during a house clearance in 2010 Bowerman's daughter-in-law, Melissa, found the actual waffle iron her late father ruined in 1970, and presented it to Nike. It seems Bill really *did* cook up a load of molten latex in his kitchen before using it to create a high-traction running shoe and—as a welcome byproduct—one of the world's most successful companies.

Now see what you think of this creation myth by John Simmons. It describes a tense moment in the real-life history of Guinness, when Dublin's civic authorities tried to block the company's access to the city's water supply—important stuff for any brewer. Look at the language, in particular the unusual word choices ("expletives," "sanctify," "girth") and the wordplay

top: Bill Bowerman, one of the prime movers behind Nike.

above: Innocent company rule book, which in typical Innocent fashion doesn't contain any rules.

The Founder's Tale from Guinness, home of
the story told here.

("stout gentleman"—Guinness is of course a stout).
Look at the structure, in particular how it begins in the
middle of the action (a technique we recommended
back in Lesson Three). It's not what you'd expect from
a big corporate, yet the result works wonderfully well
and illustrates the difference between a dry history
and an engaging brand narrative:

> The story starts with the expletives deleted. We don't
> need to sanctify the memory of our founder but no
> one ever recorded the swear words Arthur Guinness
> flung across the barricades at the gentlemen from
> the Dublin Corporation in 1775. But fling them he did.
>
> The temptation is to describe Arthur Guinness as
> a stout gentleman. Well, we make no point about his
> girth but we do know Arthur Guinness took his time
> before he came around to brewing porter. When he
> finally did, it was worth waiting for.

This microstory explains that Honda's
Swindon factory is back in action, and that
means good times for local businesses.
Notice how they're promoting a brand,
not a product.

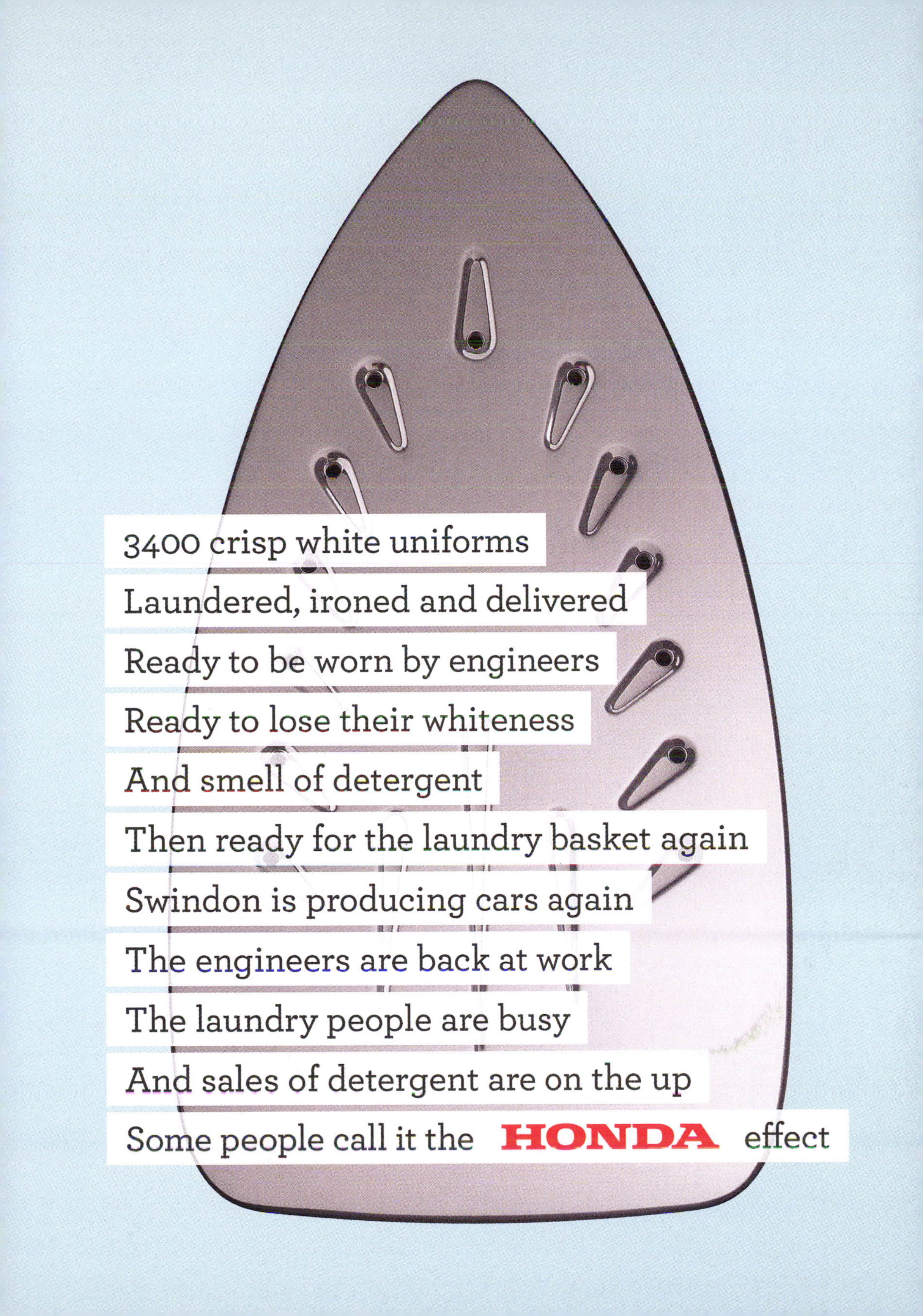

3400 crisp white uniforms

Laundered, ironed and delivered

Ready to be worn by engineers

Ready to lose their whiteness

And smell of detergent

Then ready for the laundry basket again

Swindon is producing cars again

The engineers are back at work

The laundry people are busy

And sales of detergent are on the up

Some people call it the **HONDA** effect

This inviting TV ad for Honda is based on a true story. One of Honda's lead engineers— a chap called Kenichi Nagahiro—hated diesel engines because they were smelly, noisy, and bad for the environment. So when he was asked to design one he took the opportunity to create something much kinder on the eyes, ears, and nose—not to mention nature.

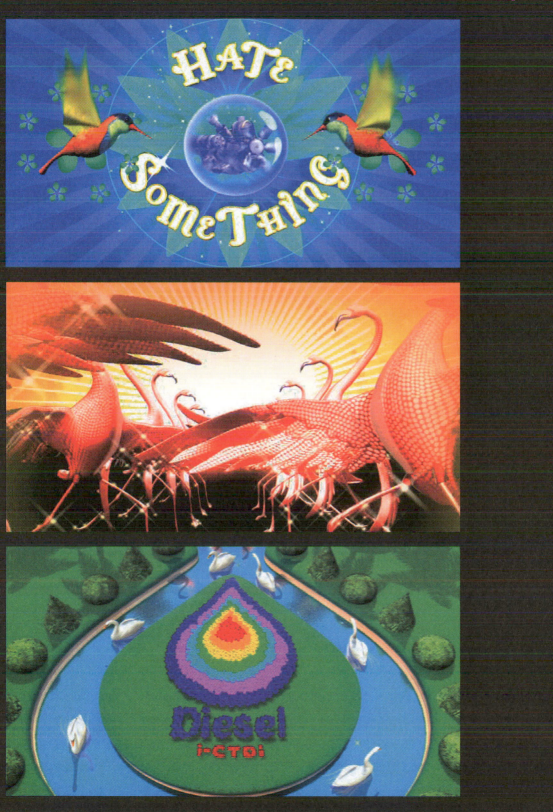

But it was water that did it. The whole history of Guinness is built on water.

Think of that the next time you sink a pint. If Arthur hadn't made his first stand against the bureaucrats and stood up for his commercial rights we wouldn't be here now thinking of new ways to fight the Guinness cause.

"I did a deal, dammit, so let's stick to it!"

Arthur Guinness stuck to it. It took him twelve years to win his fight for the Dublin water rights, but he won. And that was the first crucial turning point in the story of Guinness.

It takes strength to do it. Not necessarily the girder-lifting strength of a strongman, but the commitment that comes with an inner certainty.

Think about it. Savour it. And lift your glass to Arthur. We owe it to him.

Founding stories like this are effective because they humanize a brand's beginnings. They describe how one or more spirited individuals overcame adversity to achieve fortune and glory, so they're about belief, vision, and maybe a little drama. In other words, they talk about business in nonbusiness terms. This ability to create emotional resonance is the brand story's greatest asset. We read and remember because we enjoy. No wonder stories are such effective communication tools.

Lucy Sweet

If you want to be a writer, here's what I have learned after 20 years of being a journalist/author/copywriter. And I don't say this as someone who has reached a point of arrival. Even when you're at the top of your professional game you will never stop learning.

1. Man up. It takes a tough cookie not to mind your work being torn to bits and reconstructed from scratch. Deal with it, it will happen everyday.

2. What you think is good/acceptable may not be to others. You might love your fiber-optic Santa Claus, but it might make other people roll their eyes and stick their fingers down their throats. Same goes for words. Think about your writing objectively, from the reader's point of view.

3. Look around you. Writers don't exist in a vacuum. Read books, consume media, be a fan of other people's work (but don't copy it). Talk to other writers. They'll probably be able to give you better advice than this.

4. Enjoy it. Words are beautiful! Be creative, and weave them together to create wonderful new worlds. Whether it's a leaflet or a novel, every word is important. If you love writing, people will want to read your work.

5. Just do it. Be there, everyday, and don't give up. Develop your writing like Rocky developed his muscles—I'm thinking a shot of you sitting at the laptop with sweat dripping onto your keyboard. OK? GO! DO IT NOW! WRITE SOMETHING!

Lucy Sweet was born in Hull in 1972 but she hasn't let that stop her. Her first writing job was for *Melody Maker* aged 19, and since then she has been a freelance journalist, writing columns and features for such diverse publications as the *Sunday Express*, *Daily Record*, *Glamour*, *The Guardian*, *New Statesman*, and *Reveal*. She is also the author of two novels published by Corgi, as well as the creator of *Chica*, an award-winning magazine for girls, and *Unskinny*, a cartoon anthology published by Quartet. After three years as an advertising copywriter, Lucy now writes about parenting, luxury travel, and fashion for the Web, and is the author of the *2013 Louis Vuitton Guide to Glasgow*.

Every brand has one

Just as every organization has a brand (a point we'll expand on in the next lesson), so every brand has a story—probably many, many stories. Making a conscious effort to tell these tales in an appropriate way isn't PR puffery, it's an effective way for a company to connect with its public and make itself understood, remembered, and maybe even liked.

The key point for copywriters is that a well-chosen story gives a brand something worthwhile to say. That's true for both business-to-business and business-to-consumer communications (often shortened to B2B and B2C). After all, business customers are still human and make buying decisions for emotional as well as rational reasons despite what they might say—stories just help them decide. The lesson is simple: if you're stuck for an angle, search for a story.

Find, don't invent

So how do you go about writing a brand story? The short answer is, you don't. You can't really *create* stories like these, you can only *uncover* them.

To do that you need to dig until you find an anecdote with reader appeal that says something worthwhile about your subject. This digging—the sort of thing journalists do every day—can feel like a thankless task; the only good news is that because you find rather than invent brand stories, if/when you strike lucky, then what you've found must be true.

The point is, stories like the Innocent creation myth are unlikely to be just sitting there waiting to be noticed. It's doubtful that during your first meeting with a client they'll blurt out something quirky and fascinating about how the business began, or how their latest product came to be. By all means ask outright if they've anything approaching a suitable story—you might get lucky. However, the chances are you'll have to do some serious research, which in practice means speaking to lots of people and panning for gold in their replies.

Even that apparently simple process can be fraught with difficulties. If you're inexperienced or lack clout with the client then getting access to knowledge holders can be hard. Your best bet is to enlist the support of a senior figure. Explain what you're trying to do, why it matters, and how they can help by pointing you in the right direction. Ideally you can use their name to get the attention of hard-to-reach members of staff, perhaps using a subject line like "XXXX suggested I get in touch" for your introductory e-mail. Explain why you need their help and how important their contribution might be. A touch of mild flattery never goes amiss.

Iain Aitch

The instruction that writers should avoid clichés has, naturally, become a cliché itself. It is a maxim with so many exceptions that apply to anyone with wit or a sense of style that it has performed a very special kind of literary self-immolation.

The accompanying plea that you should "write about what you know" has, however, never been more relevant. Every form of writing, from novels to Web content, and from ad copy to journalism, can benefit from your voice, your knowledge, your tastes, and your authority.

This doesn't mean sticking "I" into the copy at every opportunity. If we wanted to read about you that much we would look at your Facebook timeline and flick through the 874 pictures of yourself that you have tagged.

What you need to instill in your writing is that element of your character that makes you memorable, makes your mates keep inviting you out, and makes your partner tell you they love you every so often. Others may put this special something down to your winning smile, your effortless charm, or your sense of humor, but the truth is that it's closer to something that the religious (myself not among them) may call your soul. It is the thing that makes you—and your writing—unique.

So every time you read back what you have written, ask yourself, "Have I put something of myself into this?" If the answer is "no" then edit and rewrite until you can honestly say "yes." Any fool can type. But writing takes soul. Your own.

Iain is a journalist and author based in London. He's written two books for major publishers, along with articles for *The Times*, *Financial Times*, *Daily Telegraph*, and *The Guardian* (where his piece on rockney legends Chas 'n' Dave was voted Article of the Year by readers). Iain is the London editor for achingly hip *Dwell* magazine, and has contributed to *Art World*, *American Craft*, *Coast*, *Dazed & Confused*, *Livingetc*, *Olive*, *Vegetarian Living*, *The Idler*, and *Bizarre*. Iain writes copy for a number of corporate clients and is an enthusiastic blogger.

Story checklist

You've found a candidate story—congratulations. Now ask yourself:

- Is it interesting, memorable, and believable?
- Could someone recognize the brand based on just the story?
- Is it right for the brand's audience? Will they get it?

If you can answer "yes" to all three then you're onto something.

Turning descriptions into stories

What do you do if you really can't find a story to suit your purposes? You do the next best thing, which is to turn a straight description into an intriguing tale. How do you do that? Here's how.

Consider the following chunk of text borrowed from an imaginary webpage for an imaginary chain of upmarket supermarkets:

We aim to develop our people at every opportunity. We've a fantastic track record of helping staff improve their skills through accredited training courses in everything from butchery to baking, produce to personnel, and management to marketing. This creates a breadth and depth of experience that keeps our customers coming back.

It's the sort of thing you see all the time in the corporate world. The from/to device—repeated three times—gives the piece a decent structure and shows the breadth of the company's business. It's perfectly well written, yet we sense a missed opportunity. Surely some or all of it could have been presented in story format for added impact? With that in mind here's our reworked version:

We do everything we can to help our staff become the best they can be. For example, we made sure Ben Jones in our Oxford store had the opportunity to train as a Master Butcher, which meant he could proudly display his graduation certificate as proof of his expertise, which meant Mrs. Lynn Manning decided to buy her meat from us this week instead of her usual butcher, which meant her husband Malcolm had some expertly trimmed pork chops for his dinner, which meant no gristly bits for Musky, their Jack Russell terrier. Sorry, boy!

We're certainly not suggesting this remix is *the* solution; instead we're saying that by making it specific, human-orientated, and image-intensive it becomes more storylike, with all the benefits that brings.

It's the same with this (fictional) paragraph taken from (fictional) MajorMining Corp's website:

Think about the electronics in your home. The chances are they include metals and minerals mined by us. That includes copper for circuit boards, gold for connectors, and silicates and rare metals used in microelectronics. At MajorMining we locate and refine the raw materials that make modern life possible.

Like the supermarket piece above it's adequate but underwhelming. And again, like the earlier example it can be usefully reworked into something more storylike, in this case by introducing human-interest specifics that show how MajorMining's products are an unseen part of everyday life:

That call you made to wish your mom Happy Birthday—we found and refined the copper that made it possible. Your train journey to work—zinc from our mine in Canada keeps the engine's chassis rust-free. Your new laptop? It wouldn't work without the rare metal palladium from our site in Australia. Your TV and DVD player? Us again. Your kids' game console, your partner's tablet device, your car's electronics...well, you get the idea. We are MajorMining, and what we do makes modern life possible.

Our point is that most organizations' copy feels flat because it fails to establish any sort of one-to-one connection with its readers. As a result there's nothing to engage the emotions or fire the imagination. That's a mistake. Strip away the hoopla and all businesses are just one group of people doing stuff for another group of people—human to human. Put it like that and presenting an organization's story *as a story* makes perfect sense. In fact it's crazy to do anything else.

No. 2ism.
The Avis Manifesto.

We are in the rent a car business, playing second fiddle to a giant.

Above all, we've had to learn how to stay alive.

In the struggle, we've also learned the basic difference between the No. 1's and No. 2's of the world.

The No. 1 attitude is: "Don't do the wrong thing. Don't make mistakes and you'll be O.K."

The No. 2 attitude is: "Do the right thing. Look for new ways. Try harder."

No. 2ism is the Avis doctrine. And it works.

The Avis customer rents a clean, new Plymouth, with wipers wiping, ashtrays empty, gas tank full, from an Avis girl with smile firmly in place.

And Avis itself has come out of the red into the black.

Avis didn't invent No. 2ism. Anyone is free to use it.

No. 2's of the world, arise!

© AVIS RENT A CAR SYSTEM, INC.

Classic ads from Avis. Note how writer Julian Koenig uses detail to create appeal—it's the classic "tell it to sell it" combo. The closing couplet of "Go with us next time. The line at our counter is shorter" must be one of the

Avis is only No.2 in rent a cars. So why go with us?

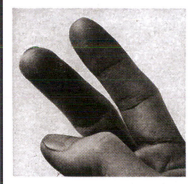

We try damned hard.

(When you're not the biggest, you have to.)

We just can't afford dirty ash-trays. Or half-empty gas tanks. Or worn wipers. Or unwashed cars. Or low tires. Or anything less than seat-adjusters that adjust. Heaters that heat. Defrost-ers that defrost.

Obviously, the thing we try hardest for is just to be nice. To start you out right with a new car, like a lively, super-torque Ford, and a pleasant smile. To know, say, where you get a good pastrami sandwich in Duluth.

Why?

Because we can't afford to take you for granted.

Go with us next time.

The line at our counter is shorter.

She was behind me when I started the band.

Behind me when I won my first fight.

Behind me when I aced my exams.

Behind me when I turned down college.

Behind me when I got our record deal.

Behind me when I chose not to fight.

Behind me when I quit the band.

Behind me when I took the job.

Behind me when her parents weren't.

Behind me when I wanted a small wedding.

Behind me when I wanted a big party.

Behind me when I wanted a 52" screen.

Behind me when I mortgaged the house.

Behind me when I started the company.

Behind me when I had the operation.

Behind me when my father died.

Behind me when my partners split.

Behind me when I nearly quit.

Behind me when I restored the business.

Behind me when I re-formed the band.

Behind me when I overtook the bus.

I saw you on the 16.51 from Finsbury Park to Brixton.
You were the redhead wearing a long pink scarf, or maybe it was just more of your hair?
You were quite short, but you could've been tall and just sitting down.
You were definitely carrying a dog and /or handbag and /or child.
If this sounds like you, call me. I was the guy who walked into the doors.

A lovely little story for an opticians that makes its point with economy and charm. Can't you just see it (no pun intended)?

Should've gone to Specsavers?

David Sandhu

These three nuggets of practical advice will hopefully serve you well:

Clients don't always know best when it comes to creative (and it's quite annoying when they do). That means you'll need the confidence to stand by your concepts and your copy (assuming they're good enough, of course) but, just as importantly, you'll need to know when it's counterproductive to argue your case. This judgment will come in time—there's no substitute for experience.

Play it simple. Don't try too hard when it comes to the actual words. It's tempting to use the big words, the clever phrasing, the copywriting equivalent of the "Hollywood Ball"... but you often won't need it. Sometimes, the hardest thing can be accepting that the easiest solution is the right solution.

Finally, remember that Woody Allen quote: "90 percent of success is just showing up." So make sure you do. On time.

David began his writing career at super-trendy style magazines *The Face* and *i-D* during the 1990s, alongside some glamorous travel writing for *Condé Nast Traveller* and the *Sunday Telegraph*, among others. Today he's an award-winning copywriter and brand consultant who specializes in corporate tone of voice and works for global clients and advertising/design agencies across the UK.

opposite top: it's impossible to read Vespa's cool, evocative copy and not start filling in the gaps to create our own personalized story of a life less ordinary.

Vespa

Our ride

La Dolce Vita

I HAVE A PROBLEM. I'm going to die. Soon.

But before I do, I have to tell you something and I'd like you to listen very carefully. After all, dying is like living – you only get one chance. So you'd better not screw up.

The thing is, I've been around. I've seen a lot. You can say what you want about Precambrian, but this has been a happening time. I've crossed the seven primordial seas, had a girl in every port. If you know what I mean.

Sure, it hasn't always been easy. There were stormy times, too, and more than once my existence hung by a thread. But no matter where I was or what went on, I always knew that my life had meaning. That I was a part of something bigger than myself.

Big words for an amoeba, you're probably thinking. Back in the old days, I might have sicced my three trillion brothers on you for that. But now my time is running out and I don't want any trouble.

I just want you to know how wonderful life is when you embrace a few simple ground rules.

Respect your swarm.

Protect the oceans — this is the only world we have.

Never get involved with plankton. I've seen more than a few good amoebas go bad that way.

But most of all enjoy life.

Stories in Oil

Mercedes-Benz

Now you have a go

Lack of confidence is the killer when it comes to brand storytelling. Everyone involved is worried about making a fool of themselves and ruining the brand's carefully nurtured reputation. We'll have no such nonsense here. Instead we beseech you to be big, bold, and brilliant. That's a lot to ask, especially if you're a rookie, but the following exercises should get you started. As always in our world, the best way to convince doubters is with great work.

Workout One

First take a piece of real brand copy and rework it as a story. The copy can come from any source but the brand's website, particularly the "About Us" section or equivalent, is a good place to start. Industry or sector is irrelevant—instead focus on finding a reasonably detailed description of some aspect of the brand's purpose or activity. Once you've found a paragraph or three you like, try putting it/them into the first person—I or we—and add as much imaginary extra detail as you need (remember, it's only a workout). Aim for something that adopts the same human-to-human approach as our examples above.

Workout Two

Now take things further—a LOT further. In his landmark book *The Seven Basic Plots*, UK author Christopher Booker explains, well, the seven basic plots of all literature. We've summarized them below. We want you to rework your piece from Workout One using one of these while keeping as much detail as you can. *Don't play it safe*—have some fun and see how far you can take it while still retaining a useful link to your source material. At what point does the connection break down?

The seven basic plots of all literature

OVERCOMING THE MONSTER
Hero learns of a great evil threatening the land and sets out to destroy it. Examples: *Terminator, Jaws, The Magnificent Seven*, any James Bond, any monster/slasher movie.

TRAGEDY
The flip side of "Overcoming the Monster." Our character is the villain, and we watch as he slides into darkness before being finally defeated, freeing the land from his evil influence. Examples: *Hamlet, Macbeth, The Lord of the Rings, Dr. Jekyll and Mr. Hyde*.

REBIRTH
Like the "Tragedy" plot, but the main character manages to realize his error before it's too late, thus avoiding inevitable defeat. Examples: *Star Wars, Sleeping Beauty, Snow White*.

LOSER TO WINNER
Surrounded by dark forces who suppress and ridicule him, the hero slowly blossoms into a mature figure who ultimately gets riches, a kingdom, and the perfect mate. Examples: "Rudolph the Red-Nosed Reindeer," Harry Potter, *David Copperfield, Cinderella, Aladdin*.

THE QUEST
Our hero learns of some lost beautiful thing he desperately wants to find, and sets out to find it, often with companions. Examples: *The Hobbit, Watership Down*, any *Indiana Jones*, anything to do with the Grail legend.

VOYAGE AND RETURN
Our hero heads off into a magic land with crazy rules, ultimately triumphs over the madness/badness he finds there, and returns home a little wiser than when he set out. Examples: *Alice in Wonderland, The Wizard of Oz, Where the Wild Things Are*, pretty much any *Dr Who* episode.

COMEDY
Hero and heroine are destined to get together but a dark force prevents them from doing so. Somehow the dark force repents and the hero and heroine are free to get together, at which point everyone is revealed as who they really are, allowing other relationships to form. Examples: *Four Weddings and a Funeral, Much Ado About Nothing*, anything by Jane Austen.

Lesson Seven:
The Brand's in Your Hands

What every copywriter needs to know about the B word

Rock paintings from "The Cave of the Hands" in Santa Cruz, Argentina. For the makers, their hand was literally their brand.

Without an appealing personality expressed in appropriate language, even the strongest brand will struggle to create an emotional connection with its audience. This matters because only one brand can be the cheapest; the rest have to find some other way of capturing their audience's attention and earning their affection. Good writing is a great way of doing exactly that.

What do we mean by "brand"? It's not as obvious as it sounds. Apple undoubtedly qualifies, as do the likes of Mercedes, L'Oréal, and Gap. But what about Lady Gaga? Or Damien Hirst? What about Belgium, Greenpeace, al-Qaida, or Harvard? Are you a brand? Why? Or alternatively, why not?

We need to get to the bottom of brands because as copywriters the chances are we'll spend most of our careers working with them. On the surface we're here to sell ideas, products, or services, but our deeper mission is almost certainly to build brands. As we pointed out earlier, in many ways it makes sense to call what we do "brandwriting" rather than "copywriting."

And that's where the problems start, for "brand" defies easy definition. We've all got an intuitive idea of what it means, but putting that into words can be surprisingly tricky. So without further ado, let's look at three definitions that illuminate different aspects of this elusive issue.

Definition one—names and logos

Here's a valiant attempt to define "brand," courtesy of the American Marketing Association:

> *A name, term, design, symbol, or any other feature that identifies one seller's goods or service as distinct from those of other sellers.*

So for the AMA a brand is a means of differentiation. That's certainly true, but it's a somewhat limited interpretation. It works well enough for consumer items like cereals or soap powder, but where does it leave the likes of plucky Belgium? High and dry, that's where. No, in many cases the brand = logo equation lacks real explaining power.

Definition two—what you do and how you do it

Interbrand—the global branding business and Gyles's erstwhile employer—define "brand" thus:

> *A mixture of attributes, tangible and intangible, symbolized in a trademark, which, if managed properly, creates value and influence.*

That's a big step in the right direction. The implication is that a brand is more than a logo, it's also an attitude, a way of doing things, an aura that surrounds a person,

place, or thing. Interbrand's definition suggests that, with the right presentation and management, more or less anything can become a brand.

So the answer to the various questions posed in the opening paragraph of this lesson is a great big "yes"— all those entities either are or have the potential to be brands. Lady Gaga doesn't have a logo as such (certainly not in the same way as Coca-Cola, with its rigorously policed corporate identity), but no one would deny she's a mega-brand. Put it like that and it's clear that "brand" is a flexible concept, able to embrace almost anything.

 You could argue that if everything is a brand then nothing is, in the sense that as soon as the advantage offered by brand status is available to all then it's no longer an advantage—instead it's just the new normal. It's possible this infinite elasticity will prove to be the brand's undoing, and in the future we'll have to invent some new way of thinking about the world. But that's another book.

Definition three—promises and expectations

Hang around with brands for long enough and you're sure to hear the phrase, "A brand is a promise." Here's what it means. Buyers tend to have certain expectations of their purchases, thanks to the endless marketing messages they're obliged to digest. BMW? Why, it's the Ultimate Driving Machine. Budweiser? We think you'll find it's the King of Beers. These slogans are claims, but they're also promises. They're saying, "Buy me and look what you'll get!, The ULTIMATE Driving Machine!, The KING of Beers!, We promise it!" So not unnaturally, people expect their purchases to deliver.

What happens next is that the brand's claim gets tested in real life, which turns the promise into experience, either good or bad. What's more, that experience sets future expectations, so if Driver A agrees that his latest BMW really *is* the Ultimate Driving Machine, it's now incumbent on BMW to make sure the next model he buys is just as good, if not better. If, three years down the line, Driver A decides his replacement Beemer is merely a Moderately Good Driving Machine then the promise has been broken.

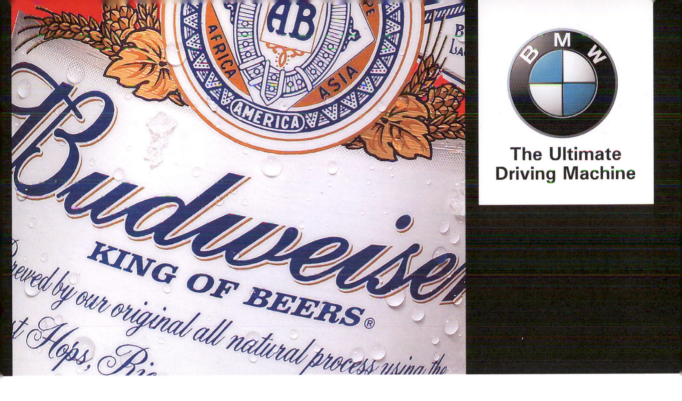

 Beware of "experience" creep

There's a tendency in modern marketing to describe everything in terms of experience, in much the same way as there's a tendency to describe everything as a brand. It ain't necessarily so. When a hungry shopper visits a supermarket they want sausages for their supper, not an extruded pork experience. To misuse language in this way weakens and debases "experience," turning a useful concept into a useless cliché. Listen carefully and you can hear Orwell tutting from beyond the grave.

The crucial thing to remember is that, strange as it may sound, *the brand owner doesn't own the brand.* They own it in a legal sense of course, but the thing that makes the brand powerful—its reputation, its aura, *its promise*—is 100 percent in the hands of its audience. It's the difference between how we describe ourselves and how others describe us. As Jeff Bezos, founder of Amazon, has remarked:

"Your brand is what people say about you when you're not in the room." [1]

We could add any number of extra definitions, for example a brand is a channel, a brand is a conversation, a brand is a relationship.... This profusion of descriptions only underscores our earlier point that "brand" can mean virtually anything. The ideas we've presented here—that brands are more than their logos, they're largely about intangible appeal, and they're ultimately owned by their audiences—are an excellent foundation.

1. Another fine Bezos brand quote is, "A brand for a company is like a reputation for a person. You earn reputation by trying to do hard things well." Similar point, different language.

Writing for brands

Clearly all sorts of things can prevent a brand from delivering on its promise, leading to nasty things being said behind its back. Almost all of them are outside the copywriter's control—it might be poorly designed, badly made, too expensive, last season's color, and so on. We're not entirely powerless, however, and our biggest contribution comes from writing about the brand in a way that encourages attraction.

So how do we do this? How do we turn an ordinary brand into a love brand, one for which audiences feel real affection? The answer is we **make a personal connection** with our readers, because that gives us the opportunity to **create an appealing personality**, which in turn enables us to **create significant difference**.

Make a personal connection

It's often said that "people buy people"—in other words, what closes a sale is the man or woman making the pitch, not the mute product or service being pitched. OK, if whatever you're selling happens to enjoy some overwhelming technical or price advantage then the logic changes, but in many cases a sale is the result of some sort of human-to-human interaction—in other words, a personal connection. And that means introducing some emotion.

The emotional trumps the rational because it allows people to *identify*—whenever someone describes themselves as "an Apple obsessive" or "a Nike addict" that's exactly what's going on. These emotional connections are about how we see ourselves and the tribe we belong to (or aspire to belong to). Our job as writers is to support this process, using language in a way that encourages readers to join the club by aligning themselves with whatever brand we're promoting. We're *not* suggesting you discount the rational—if you've got solid reasons for the reader to buy/believe/whatever then work your facts hard. Instead

Apple's "I'm a Mac and I'm a PC" is pure "personality as difference." They're exaggerating for effect but there's more than a grain of truth in there.

we're saying take an enlightened approach that acknowledges the importance of emotions and uses all the material at your disposal to its maximum effect.

Create an appealing personality

This emotional dimension often comes from the tone we use—in other words, the personality we create in our writing. What we're talking about here is *verbal identity*[2], the way a brand conjures up a clear and meaningful personality for itself using words alone. This process is driven by *values,* the principles[3] and beliefs a brand claims to hold dear. It's just common sense—if someone or something behaves in a way that somehow matches our personal beliefs then there's a decent chance of a bond developing.

So while not exactly simple, the copywriter's challenge is straightforward: we need to make the brands we write about likeable by imbuing them with characteristics that are both appropriate (in the sense that they genuinely reflect the brand's values) and appealing (in the sense that they attract the right audience, and keep them close once they've been drawn in).

Use personality to create difference

So far we've established that an emotional connection is the basis of much effective copywriting, and that a brand's verbal identity helps create and sustain that connection. This process becomes even more significant when we consider that brands are in competition with each other, yet the products or services they represent are often strikingly similar (if you're lucky enough to be writing about something with a genuine point of difference then happy days).

In this situation the personality you create for a brand can make a decisive contribution to its success. What you're really doing is *creating difference*, and not just any difference—this is *appealing* difference *that makes a difference*.

The good news is we're pre-programmed to find difference, as Jeremy Bullmore has noted:

> *The human mind both abhors and rejects the concept of parity. Give a small boy two identical marbles and within an hour he will have formed a preference for one.*

So our job is to help our readers form the right preference by giving our brand an attractive personality and bringing that personality to life in a way that appeals to people. The result will stand out in a sea of sameness.

---

2. Verbal identity is essentially the same as tone of voice. For us the difference—such as it is—centers on application. Verbal identity is an expression or description of a brand's on-page personality, whereas tone of voice is about the actual words a brand uses in ads and so on.

3. One of advertising's greatest figures—Bill Bernbach—once pronounced, "A principle isn't a principle until it costs you money." It's a great line and a nice idea, but how many businesses actually follow their principles/values in this way?

Like any successful brand, British Airways uses its advertising to project a distinct personality that helps it stand out in a crowded market. Compare its comms to those from other airlines and you'll see what we mean.

Kim Mok

I think back to when I was just starting out in this industry: a fresh, young creative assistant happily (or fake-happily) running out to get coffee twice a day and picking up dry cleaning on the way back, dreaming of future advertising glory.

And I have words for that girl.

Silly twit, I would say as I not-so-gently shake her shoulders. When acquaintances ask you how you've been, try not to vomit up a monologue on the complexities of your latest retail ad.

When your parents ask you what exactly it is you do for a living, don't rant to them about awards shaped like writing instruments or wild animals.

Also, saying you're watching something just to see the commercials is like saying you only read *Playboy* for the articles...but really meaning it.

If you think only about advertising, talk only about advertising, study only advertising, and hang out only with advertising people, you will be a huge bore.

Do not be a bore.

It's not good for you. It's not good for the people that have to sit next to you at dinner parties. And it's definitely not good for your creativity—which means it's not even good for your career.

Take a foreign language class for no reason. Go on a solo trip to an exotic country. Wander around and get lost in your own city. Enrol in a cooking class on donut making. Fail that cooking class.

Just do not be a bore.

And, by the way, no matter how high and mighty you may eventually think you are, remember you used to be that assistant with the dopey grin and coffee stains down the front of her shirt.

Kim has done hard time at an impressive range of top US ad agencies, including Droga5, BBDO, and TBWA\Chiat\Day. Along the way she's garnered an equally impressive range of awards and curiously shaped mantelpiece adornments. Today she's a brilliantly capable creative director based in New York with—to quote one of her colleagues—"solid digital chops." We're not 100 percent sure what that means but it sounds mighty impressive.

FROM PERSONAL TO PURCHASE

MAKE IT PERSONAL

...in order to...

CREATE PERSONALITY

...in order to...

CREATE DIFFERENCE

...because...

DIFFERENCE IS THE BASIS
OF PREFERENCE

...and...

PREFERENCE IS THE FIRST
STEP TO PURCHASE

Making it happen

Putting this into practice means returning to an idea first mentioned in our lesson on audiences—"Whose voice should we hear when we read the words?" We said this is a key question—perhaps *the* key question —to ask when searching for the right voice for a particular readership. It's equally relevant here.

To understand why, we need to acknowledge that reading begins with listening. As our eyes track along a line of text the squiggles of ink they encounter aren't magically transformed into thoughts, memories, and so on. Instead they have to go through an intermediate stage where they take the form of inner dialogue (or "silent speech," as cognitive psychologists call it). Children often move their lips in time with this silent speech; adults—even art directors usually don't. So reading is really the act of listening to this silent speech as it plays out in our head.

Our point is that this silent speech can have just as much personality as normal speech. If the copywriter is sufficiently skillful then the inner dialogue their words create will have all the traits of the most evocative vocal speech. In fact they're essentially the same thing, it's just that one is internal and the other external.

Achieving all this is agreeably easy. To exploit inner dialogue's ability to create personality, simply picture a real-life individual with the same traits as the brand you're dealing with, then write with their voice in mind. Essentially this individual becomes your voice model.

It's like an actor getting into character as preparation for a performance. And just like an actor, the most effective way for a copywriter to understand the voice of their character is through research. If your model is a public figure, then find some online videos of them in action and create a list of their verbal mannerisms. How do they speak? What unusual turns of phrase do they use? How do they start a sentence? Or end one? How do they express pleasure? Or dissatisfaction? What do they always say? What would they never say? And so on. Make a list, the more detailed the better.

It's exactly the same if the individual you're modeling isn't in the public realm, although obviously you can't rely on YouTube. In this situation you could use a number of public figures as references sources and build up a sort of composite description of the voice you're after, taking different mannerisms from different individuals. Either way, you need to reach a point where you've a clear idea of how your brand would speak if it were this person. It's then a reasonably straightforward job to give your copy instant personality by merging these verbal mannerisms with your raw material.

Recently Roger used this approach to good effect while writing for a charity that looks after some of London's most historic landmarks. The client had identified a popular TV historian as the voice of the brand, so Roger was able to quickly build up a list of the historian's verbal tics and use them to enliven the client's source text. The result had plenty of personality and took hours rather than days to create. Try this technique yourself—it works.

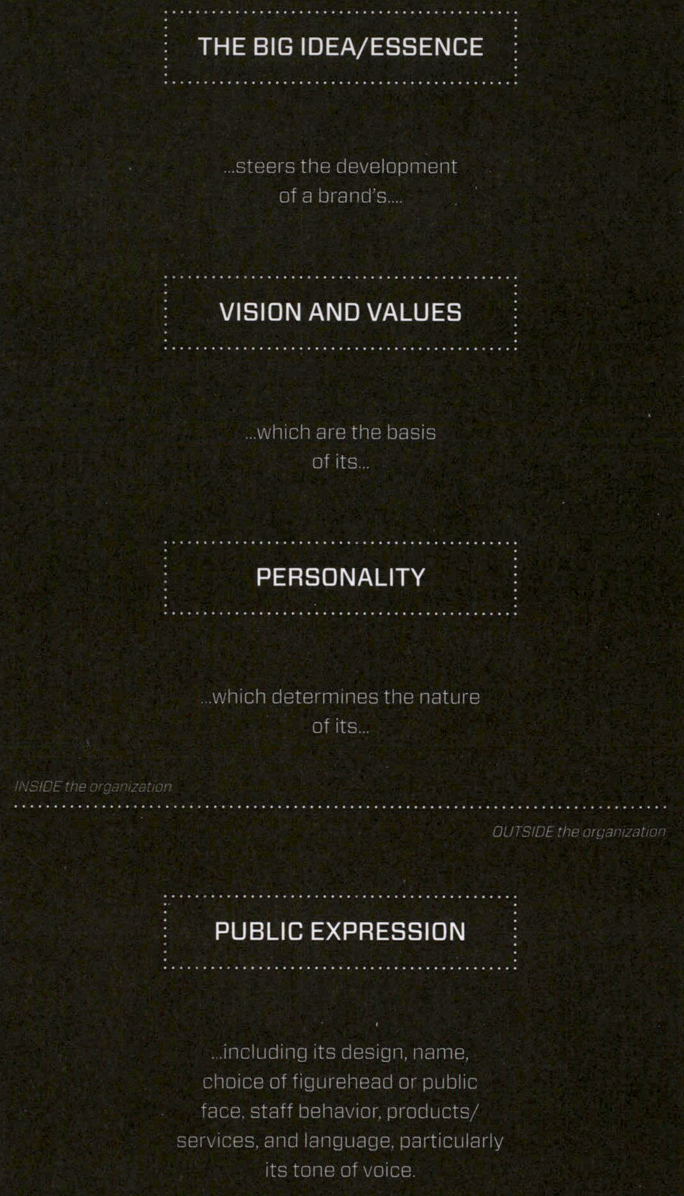

THE BIG IDEA/ESSENCE

...steers the development
of a brand's....

VISION AND VALUES

...which are the basis
of its...

PERSONALITY

...which determines the nature
of its...

INSIDE the organization

OUTSIDE the organization

PUBLIC EXPRESSION

...including its design, name,
choice of figurehead or public
face, staff behavior, products/
services, and language, particularly
its tone of voice.

How a brand's various components work together.

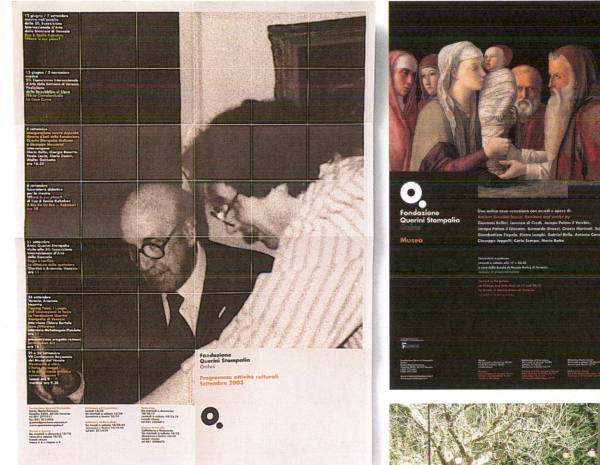

This clean, uncluttered identity for Venetian cultural institution Fondazione Querini Stampalia shows how a small number of brand elements can be used in all manner of ways across all manner of media.

Halifax makes a feature of their staff in their ads. It's a tried-and-true approach, and part of their brand.

Brand basics

Before we end let's take a quick spin through the nuts and bolts of brands. Digest what follows and you'll be able to talk branding with the best of them.

Brand components

A **big idea** or **essence** is the central thought that captures a brand's main point of difference. It's often a single word or short phrase. In his book, *The Big Idea*, UK brand expert Robert Jones writes that Apple's essence is "different" while management consultants McKinsey & Company's is "rigor."

A brand's **values** refer to the principles it lives by, usually expressed as a series of adjectives. At the time of writing, HSBC's values are "open," "connected," and "dependable." Values are, in effect, a set of benchmarks that brands use to define their behavior, although how many genuinely allow their values to steer their corporate conduct is hard to say. In many cases it might make more sense to talk about "aspirations" rather than values; however, let's not get sidetracked.

Next, a brand's vision describes its ambition for the future. Early in its life Nike's vision was reportedly to "Crush Adidas," while Heinz were guided by the considerably less macho, "To be the world's premier food company, offering nutritious, superior-tasting foods to people everywhere."

Finally, a brand's personality refers to the human character traits a brand adopts to make itself likeable and relevant. Nokia define their brand personality (and, by extension, their tone of voice) as "authentic," "sociable," "curious," and "enthusiastic."

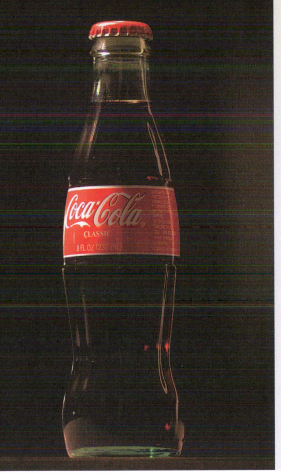

Iconic design is the basis of these brands.

Brand expression

Design

This refers to logos, color palettes, typefaces, photography, and illustrations, and the rules governing their use. These elements come together to form what's sometimes called an "identity system"—the totality of visual elements that represent a particular brand. Most identity systems are rigid (in the sense that there's a single logo and so on, with very definite rules governing its use); others—for example Tate Galleries in London, the MIT Media Lab in Massachusetts, or the City of Melbourne in Australia— have scope for variation in their design and art direction.

Names

Brand names come in a number of fruity flavors. They can be descriptive (Toys R Us), evocative (Amazon), or superlative (Mr Muscle). They can borrow from a place connected with the product or service in question (*Wall Street Journal*, Singapore Airlines), they can use the founder's surname (Ferrari), first name (Ben &

Jerry's), or a group name (Quaker Oats). They can be an abbreviation (Intel, FedEx), an acronym (BBC, KFC), or a neologism (Prozac, Xerox, Kodak). The main thing to know is that brand naming can be a tricky business and despite what some agencies might say, intuition counts as much as method when it comes to picking a winner.

Figurehead or public face

These come in two broad types: those with a genuine connection to the brand (the late Steve Jobs for Apple, Sir Richard Branson for Virgin), and those who're paid to stand in front of a camera (any actor or celebrity fronting any campaign). The former isn't necessarily more effective than the latter—it's fair to say Bill Gates was never a particularly persuasive advocate for Microsoft, despite the fact it was basically his idea.

Staff behavior

These are the folks who actually deliver the product or service that the brand represents. As most of us know from personal experience, a surly or stupid member of

Mandy Wheeler

When you're writing for the Web: Read your work out loud.

When you're writing for radio: Read your work out loud.

When you're writing for film, TV, or animation: Read your work out loud.

When you're writing a press ad, a letter, an e-mail, a blog post, a presentation, a brochure, a press release, a proposal of marriage, or the copy for a can of beans: Read your work out loud.

It will help.

Creative Director of Punch It Up, Mandy is a writer who also runs workshops to punch up the creative output of organizations ranging from banks to the BBC, and artists to ad agencies. Before Punch It Up she ran Mandy Wheeler Sound Productions, an award-winning production company with whom she turned out a couple of thousand ads and numerous radio programs.

staff can ruin our view of an organization faster than just about anything. If they get it wrong then all the hard work and expense that goes into building a brilliant brand can be undone in seconds. Staff behavior is an incredibly important and often underappreciated part of how we experience brands.

Products and services

These are the things the brand actually represents, and clearly they have to deliver. It's sometimes said that good advertising helps a bad product fail faster. That's because it draws attention to its shortcomings and emphasizes the yawning void between a brand's promise and the actual experience it delivers.

Language

Our bit. Brand language covers everything from the brand's name and tagline/slogan, through to ads, annual reports, articles, brochures, case studies, data sheets, direct-mail pieces, flyers, leaflets, letters, newsletters, packaging, posters, presentations, scripts, signage, speeches, social media, websites, and plenty more besides. As this list suggests, words are a fundamental part of virtually all brands, which is of course what this lesson is about.

And finally...

Brands are also expressed in product design (think the classic Coca-Cola bottle or the original VW Beetle), trade dress (think UPS's brown trucks and uniforms), and sound (think Intel's four-note "flourish" or "Mmm, Danone"). On this last point we could legitimately say a country's national anthem is its sound signature (in the same way that its flag is its logo), and that a TV show's theme tune is a major part of its brand.

Now you have a go

Not surprisingly the best brandwriting happens when a brand has a distinct personality for the writer to spark off. The better you understand a brand's personality (and the voice that articulates that personality), the better your writing will be.

Workout One

We've said "Whose voice should we hear?" is an important question to ask when writing for brands. To emphasize this we'd like you to rework the following copy...

Domaine du Colombier
This gorgeous golden wine is fresh, fruity, and incredibly drinkable. Made from 100 percent Chardonnay grapes and bursting with the flavor of kiwifruit, limes, and apples, it's a classic Chablis from the rolling chalk hills of northern Burgundy. All our winemaster's years of experience have gone into selecting a wine with the ideal balance of dry finish and honeyed taste. It's part of our commitment to bring you the finest wines at the lowest prices.

...in the voice of one of the following figures:

Robert De Niro
Homer Simpson
Borat
Queen Elizabeth II
Gordon Ramsay
Fred Flintstone

There's a lot of information in the original, and you don't have to get it all in. Instead concentrate on making sure your chosen voice comes though loud and clear. Here's the clincher: Show (don't read) your work to a friend and ask them to identify the "speaker"—if they get it right without any prompting then you've succeeded. If not, you need to turn up the volume on your chosen voice.

Workout Two

Let's explore the idea that personality, expressed through language, is the basis of a brand's audience appeal.

First find a brand with strong, clear personality (you'll probably want a B2C brand as these tend to play up their personality compared to their B2B brethren).

Next describe that brand's verbal identity—a few well-chosen adjectives should do it. Now ask yourself to what extent is that identity *appropriate* given the brand's particular line of business? In other words, have they chosen wisely? Is their identity an asset or an irrelevance?

Next, to what extent is the brand's verbal identity *appealing*? Does it help attract the right audience? Could they do anything differently to increase their appeal?

Finally, how does this verbal identity create *difference*, enabling the brand to stand out from its competitors?

Lesson Eight:
A Question of Style

How figures of speech can make your sentences sing

Different expressions create
different impressions.

Way back in Lesson Three we talked about sticky writing and suggested a toolbox of techniques to help make your text tacky (in a good way). In this lesson we delve a little deeper into the mechanics of style with a sprint through the fascinating world of figures of speech.

et's start with a quick quiz. What have these three sentences got in common?

Miss Bolo...went straight home in a flood of tears and a sedan chair
Dickens in *The Pickwick Papers*

The general who became a slave. The slave who became a gladiator. The gladiator who defied an emperor. Striking story!
Commodus in Ridley Scott's *Gladiator*

You're wel-diddly-elcome!
Ned Flanders in *The Simpsons*

All three are—as if you hadn't guessed—examples of figures of speech; colorful, nonliteral turns of phrase we use to spice up our expression. The first is known as a *zeugma* (a verb or adjective applied to two or more nouns when it really applies to just one of them), the second is an *anadiplosis* (repeating the last word of a preceding clause to create a list structure), and the third is *tmesis* (splitting a word or phrase apart and inserting another word or space into the gap for dramatic or humorous effect).

Although unlikely to be useful on an hourly basis, all three show how figures of speech can give our words more color, emphasis, and impact. As Roger has written elsewhere,[1] figures can be of real benefit to copywriters. They evolved as part of the art of rhetoric, an end-to-end technique for effective communication much loved by Roman senators and the like (hence the Latinate names of many figures). The aim of rhetoric was to present a spoken argument with such power and eloquence that the audience couldn't help but be convinced. Substitute "spoken" for "written" and that's a decent definition of copywriting—hence this lesson. Having set the scene, allow us to introduce a few choice figures every copywriter would do well to know.

top: These posters invite us to picture a human in place of the poster and consider our reaction. The poster is literally a metaphor for an individual.

above: The Ramones' first-ever press release. Note the "hundred howitzers" metaphor and "fast drill on a rear molar" simile.

Metaphors and similes

Metaphor: *A word or phrase that makes an* **implicit** *comparison between two unconnected items without using "as" or "like." For example, "It's a dog-eat-dog world" or "The Lord is my shepherd."*

Simile: *A word or phrase that makes an* **explicit** *comparison between two unconnected items using either "as" or "like." For example "Happy as Larry" or "Sleep like a log."*

Word pictures—in the form of metaphors and similes—beat a straight description every time. They're tailormade to create striking images in your reader's mind and pack plenty of meaning into a minuscule space, making them useful when your word count is restricted.

For example, when Johnson & Johnson advertised a new sticking plaster with the line "Say hello to your child's new bodyguards," readers immediately understood the plaster was strong, reliable, provided protection, and would generally take care of their kids —just like a bodyguard. It's all a lot more effective than saying, "This plaster is strong, reliable, provides protection, and will generally take care of your kids— just like a bodyguard."

Likewise Jergens skincare's strapline "Science you can touch" worked because the verb "touch" isn't usually associated with an abstract concept like "science." The friction caused by the apparent mismatch of these two ideas is what gives this metaphor its heat—a useful technique to know if you're looking for a tagline.

Hyperbole

Def: *Extravagant exaggeration for effect, such as the classic "I've told you a million times not to exaggerate."*

One effective way to emphasize a point is to massively *over*-emphasize it. Your audience will know you're not describing the literal properties of your subject, but they'll be equally clear that you're alluding to something pretty exceptional. It's a curious process by which you can convince readers of a truth by deliberately overstating it.

A great example comes from Young & Rubicam in Singapore and a series of ads they created for Uhu's new super glue. One ad gave ultra-detailed instructions for the product's safe use, a second included exhaustive directions to not one but three local hospitals, while the third ad in the series read:

> ### Keep out of reach of:
> *Small children, the elderly, the infirm, your wife, your husband, your friends, your relatives, the easily distracted, the mentally challenged, hippies, yuppies, teens, tweens, luddites, drunks, the meek, that guy over there, that guy behind him, in fact all those people, guys with nicknames, guys who give their privates nicknames, girls who tolerate guys who give their privates nicknames...*

Ending, rather sensibly, on "pets." All three are heroically hyperbolic.

Chiasmus

Def: *A figure of speech made up of two clauses, the second of which reverses the first, for example "When the going gets tough, the tough get going.'*

In need of instant profundity? Then do what generations of speechwriters have done and try mirroring one part of a phrase to create a snappy comeback. The result is called a chiasmus—the figure behind Kennedy's "Ask not what your country can do for you, ask what you can do for your country" and Mae West's "It's not the men in your life that counts, it's the life in your men."

The chiasmus either presents a mirror image of a concept for the purposes of persuasion, or rebuts a point by turning it around. Along the way it makes the commonplace seem catchy. If you're stuck for a line try flipping parts of a common phrase to create something new, or try using opposites or contradictions to draw attention to or affirm your point.

If that sounds a bit complex consider these examples. The Apple iMac was originally advertised with the line "Simply amazing. Amazingly simple," while Harley-Davidson suggested we "Live to ride, ride to live." Both use the mirroring technique we've just described to make their magic.

A close cousin is the **implied chiasmus**, where words *within* a phrase are reversed to memorable effect, for example Microsoft's "You can tell a lot about a company by the people they keep." Using much the same

Translation: *Economist* readers have intelligence and nothing stimulates thought like our magazine. Which has more stick? Exactly.

"Run yourself ugly" isn't meant to be taken literally. Instead it's suggesting that sore and sweaty is just a step on the journey to the body beautiful. The tone is maintained in similiar slogans throughout this brochure for Nike.

Great minds like a think.

Classic overemphasis for effect.
We're left in no doubt as to Uhu's potency.

SETS in SECONDS!!

FOR BEST USE:

PLEASE READ ALL DIRECTIONS. WASH HANDS. CLEAN ALL SURFACES OF DIRT. TURN OFF THE TV. TURN OFF ANY MUSIC. UNPLUG THE PHONE. GET EVERYONE ELSE OUT OF THE ROOM. BREATHE DEEPLY. QUIET YOUR MIND. MAKE SURE YOU GET A GOOD NIGHT'S SLEEP. DO NOT CONSUME ANY ALCOHOL 36 HOURS BEFORE USING. FORGIVE YOUR PARENTS. COME TO TERMS WITH YOUR PAST. ACCEPT WHO YOU ARE. MAKE PEACE WITH YOUR MANY DEMONS. REALIZE THAT YOU ARE A UNIQUE BEING IN THE UNIVERSE AND ARE PART OF A PLAN GREATER THAN YOU CAN POSSIBLY IMAGINE. STORE AT ROOM TEMPERATURE.

opposite top: Pure parallelism in list format.

opposite bottom: There are two parallel features here; the repetition of "...drink it because...," and the pairing of "...it's from Texas..." with "...it's not from England."

technique, one of the many superb print ads for *The Economist* uses the line "Great minds like a think," which neatly inverts the expected "...think alike" ending.

An implied chiasmus also provides the raw material for a series of award-winning press and poster ads for courier service FedEx. These showed a pair of hands unwrapping a package containing a long-redundant piece of home technology, with the tagline "Late is as good as never," which riffs on the familiar idiom "Better late than never." The implication—that if a package doesn't arrive on time then there's no point in it arriving at all—was underscored by the signoff line "Nobody's in a bigger hurry than we are."

Parallelism

Def: *Presenting two or more parts of a sentence in a similar way to give the whole a well-defined, regular form, for example Caesar's "I came, I saw, I conquered" or Chevrolet's "Eye it, try it, buy it."*

Parallelism is the copywriter's friend. If you've got several related things to say, try looking for a consistent structure in which to say them. You can then present the results in either sentence form or as bullets. It works a treat.

Parallelism comes in various forms—the two we'll cover are the **bicolon** and the **tricolon**. Sometimes called "the rule of two" (bicolon) and "the rule of three" (tricolon), both are ready-made structures ripe for creating memorable lines.

Rule-of-two examples include Timex watches' "It takes a licking, and keeps on ticking," Nissan's "Everything you want, nothing you don't," and Nice 'n Easy Shampoo's "The closer he gets, the better you look."

Then there's this slogan for Bounce fabric softener: "Stops static before static stops you." In the first part

the noun "static" is the object of the verb "stops," while in the second it becomes the subject. The addition of alliteration only introduces extra melody to the phrase.

The rule of three is an equally powerful weapon in your persuasive arsenal. It suggests completeness in a way that a two-item couplet can't quite manage, and has a nice rhythm that a four-point approach lacks. In fact anything with four points and above is a common-or-garden list—very useful, of course, but not what we're interested in here. The group of three can work at the word level ("Location, location, location"), the phrase level ("Government of the people, by the people, for the people"), and the sentence level, as a UK print ad for Honda cars shows (see p.147):

> There is a place where dreamers go. Where crazy flights of fancy are valued above all else. Where the only good idea is an idea that's never been had before. Where dreams can become real. It's called The Patent Office, Concept House, Newport – M4, junction 28, first roundabout, fourth exit.

Without wishing to analyze the magic out of this charming paragraph,[2] the three sentences beginning with "where" create an increasing sense of expectation and excitement, which is then amusingly dashed by the Concept House comedown.

All these examples introduce a rhythm to the writing that's both attractive and practical. By making the structure of your sentences predictable (in the best possible way) you'll help your readers make sense of them. The trick, as we say, is to use grammatically equivalent phrases presented in a regular format. With a little imagination you can use parallelism to present a complex group of ideas in a way that doesn't read like a list—a useful skill for all writers.

---

2. As Wordsworth wrote, "We murder to dissect." His point was that too much analysis tends to kill whatever made something special in the first place.

I am ordinary *I am unique*
I am a darling *I am a freak*
I am How do you do *I am Who the hell are you*
I am champagne in the park *I am vodka in the dark*
I am Leicester Square's latest sensation *I am Camden Town's strangest creation*
I am the girl from next door *I am the mistress you adore*
I am sunshine *I am rain*
I am kittens *I am pain*

I am Illamasqua

ILLAMASQUA
Make-up for your alter ego

Leader's digest.

Creating a basic pun isn't hard: Find a key word, locate another that sounds alike, then swap them around—that is how this ad works, with "Leader's" standing in for "Reader's" to humorous effect.

More tricolon action. Notice how the neat three-part structure is perfect for describing a sequence of events, rather like Caesar's "I came, I saw, I conquered."

.The tricolon at work. Classic stuff.

The firefighters have cut the driver free.

The paramedics have rushed him to hospital.

The nurses have taken him to the operating theatre.

Now he's waiting for your call.

At 5.15am, the mother's water broke.

At 7.07am, the consultant performed an emergency Caesarean.

At 7.27am, she was delivered 10 weeks prematurely.

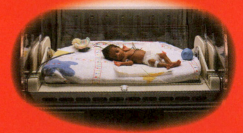

Now she's waiting for your call.

There is a place where dreamers go. Where crazy flights of fancy are valued above all else. Where the only good idea is an idea that's never been had before. Where dreams can become real. It's called The Patent Office, Concept House, Newport – M4, junction 28, first roundabout, fourth exit. Do you believe in the power of dreams?

Luke Sullivan

Anne Lamott is the author of one of my favorite books on writing—*Bird By Bird*. The title itself is one of the first lessons Anne gives us, in which she recalls having to write a long report about birds for school. She was daunted by the size of the project and finally in frustration asked her dad, "How am I ever going to *write* this?!?" And her wise father answered, "Bird by bird, Anne. Bird by bird."

And so it goes with *all* of our creative projects, be it writing, art, or film.

Creative projects *are* daunting. In fact, the more we care about a project, the scarier it is, the larger it begins to loom over the measly 24 hours available in our day. Setting out, we begin to see all the wonderful angles we might explore, and we *freeze*. We tighten up and pull back.

This is when resistance to writing usually kicks in. Happens to me all the time. In fact, the way *I* procrastinate is to "do research." Gathering material and back story may be a key part of the problem-solving process, but I use it as a crutch or, rather, a hidey-hole. *I can't possibly begin to write this! Don't you see how MUCH there is I don't know?*

Recognizing that we are indeed resisting work is the first step. So we take a deep adult breath and tell ourselves, "It's time to start, dear."

Start … OK. Fine, start … but *how*? *This* big-ass project? It's still *here*, spilled all over my desktop, its files obliterating the serene screensaver picture of the lake, the lake I'm *never* going to sit next to because of this damn project. Fine! I'll start! But where? *Where* do I start?

And again, Ms. Lamott comes to our rescue with another piece of calm and loving advice.

"Start from where you are."

Wow.

When you think about it, how can we start anywhere *else*? We have to start from here. And yet most of us want to somehow maaaaybe just think our way down the road a piece, not far, you know, maybe start mapping out the journey, just sorta get a grip on this dang thing, maybe also get the 30,000-foot view of all the different roads and, dammit, *let's solve the whole stinkin' thing right now!* And again, our mental wagon train grinds to a halt before we even start west.

"Start from where you are."

So, this is the piece of advice I have most loved. I remember using it recently while writing a book. There it sat in my computer, non-existent, completely unwritten, with different chapters all burning for immediate attention.

The thing is, there was one scene I couldn't wait to write. This particular scene was smack dab in the middle of the book. I can't start there. Can I?

And I did. I started exactly there. This scene was the part I was most *excited* about writing, which made it exactly the right place for me to pick up the project. I could worry about the opening chapters later. I could worry about the end later. But simply by picking up this one part that interested me, I was able to keep at it, to stay bent over my keyboard for the longest time; and enjoy doing it.

Thanks, Anne. And now I pass it on to you guys. See that part of your big project that's the most interesting piece? Start there.

Luke is a copywriter with over three decades' experience at some of America's leading ad agencies, including Fallon, The Martin Agency, and GSD&M. His trophy cabinet bulges with all manner of shiny awards, including over 20 medals from the prestigious One Show (advertising's equivalent of the Oscars). Originally from Minnesota, Luke now chairs the advertising department at the Savannah College of Art and Design and is the author of the quite superb *Hey Whipple, Squeeze This: The Classic Guide to Creating Great Ads*. Additionally, he just released a memoir titled *Thirty Rooms To Hide In: Insanity, Addiction, and Rock 'n' Roll in the Shadow of the Mayo Clinic*.

Puns

Def: *A playful substitution of words that sound alike but mean different things, for example the timeless, "My wife and I went on holiday to the Caribbean." "Jamaica?" "No, she went of her own accord."*

Humor is a great attractor/persuader. Puns in particular make superb sticky lines *but only if they help make the message more persuasive or memorable*. The fact we've started this section with a warning highlights the fact that caution is required. Nevertheless puns can be a brilliantly effective way to create stickiness, something every tabloid headline writer knows only too well.

You may be aware that puns have a mixed reputation; indeed some people believe they have no place in copywriting. To their detractors we say only this: when you've written something to beat the *Economist* campaign let us know. Almost entirely text-based, this long-running series of print and poster ads has employed such masterful pun-based lines as "Free enterprise with every copy," "Attracts magnates," "Honing device," and "Utter brilliance." What makes these ads so special is their (no pun intended) economy—the pun format enables their writers to pack far more into each phrase than would otherwise be possible. The result is one of the best text-based campaigns ever created.

Puns are popular with many writers for the simple reason that they're fun to create and can spice up an otherwise straight-faced piece of communication. For example, Morton Salt advertised their damp-resistant salt with the line "When it rains, it pours" (punning on the idea of different levels of downpour), only for Michelin Tyres to respond with "When it pours, it reigns" (punning on the similarity of rain/reign).

Punny chocolate packaging. Worked for us.

This ad ran in the program of the Global Leadership Forum, an international conference at which Donald Trump was the keynote speaker. History doesn't recall his reaction.

Trump Donald.

The Economist

Similarly, Corona soft drinks employed the tagline "Every bubble's passed its fizzical" (punning on the similarity of physical and fizzical), while Coca-Cola used "Coke refreshes you like no other can" (based on the double meaning of "can" as both a beverage container and an indication of possibility). *The Times* newspaper in the UK went with "Our sages know their onions," punning on the phrase "To know one's onions" (and the idea that experts are sometimes called "sages"), while More cigarettes enjoined us to "Ask for more," a pun that works by associating their brand name with the idea we shouldn't be satisfied with anything less.

Finally—and staying with the "more" theme—Durex chose to advertise their new "climax delay" condoms with the slogan "roger more" spelt out in condom-shaped lettering. This pun on the name of the ex-007 actor cheekily emphasized the key benefit of their new product—or at least it did until the UK's advertising watchdog ruled it offensive on the grounds that it might promote casual sex.[3]

Before we leave puns we should pause briefly to examine a closely related figure, the **antanaclasis** (from the Greek for "reflection" or "bending back"). This cousin of the pun involves repeating a single word but with a different meaning each time. For example Vidal Sassoon's "If you don't look good, we don't look good," Coca-Cola's "People on the go, go for Coke," and Felix cat food's "Cats like Felix like Felix." Like puns, a great technique for sticky lines of all descriptions.

From "our" to "aah," a neat switch that builds on the brand's long-standing "Aah, Bisto" tagline.

3. Apparently just three people objected. Durex complied and pulled the ads but admitted they were "perplexed by the decision."

Alliteration

Def: *The repetition of the initial sound or letter of a word, as in "It takes two to tango," "The more the merrier," "Rolls-Royce," or "Dunkin' Donuts."*

Alliteration is a simple way to create pleasing phrases out of unpromising source material. It's one of the few figures of speech taught at school (certainly in the UK) and is part and parcel of everyday language, cropping up in common idioms and phrases like, well, "part and parcel." Thanks to its ability to make the commonplace catchy, alliteration is also at the heart of many a marvelous mnemonic. If you're stuck for a snappy phrase, try adding some alliteration and see where it gets you.

Alliteration is really about repetition. The Girl Guides promote themselves with a great alliterative line: "Dream. Dare. Do." (technically speaking that's three lines but let's not get hung up on periods), Jaguar Cars issued the following challenge to US buyers: "Don't dream it. Drive it." Then there's "Maybe it's Maybelline," "If anyone can, Canon can," "You can be sure of Shell"… the list goes on.

In contrast to many of the figures we've examined, alliteration comes naturally to many writers and is perhaps the most accessible figure described here. Yet this commendable urge to add melody to our words comes with an important caveat. Although it looks simple enough, alliteration has to be deliberate to work well. Alliterate by all means, just do it with confidence.

Oxymoron and paradox

Oxymoron: *A figure of speech in which opposing or incongruous ideas are placed together to create a surprising new meaning, for example, "Cruel to be kind" or "Less is more." Often mistakenly used as a synonym for "contradiction in terms," for example "military intelligence."*

Paradox: *"A truth standing on its head to attract our attention," although you could say the same about oxymora in general (and many other figures). The main difference between the two is length—paradoxes tend to be longer and more sentence-like than oxymora.*

Both these figures are examples of what's sometimes called a "self-canceling phrase," a bright, energetic image that draws attention to its subject by opposing what we instinctively know to be true. The result jolts us into paying attention. Architect Mies van der Rohe could have described his affection for minimalism as "Simple is best" but he didn't; instead he came up with (or more correctly borrowed) "Less is more," a phrase that makes much the same point but with far more style and impact.[4]

Oxymora and paradoxes work by exploiting the power of truth, then doing the opposite of what's expected. For example, a recent "call for entries" for the Singapore Creative Circle advertising awards used exactly this approach to grab its readers' attention. As is usual with such documents, it began by asking for the:

- Nominated ad:
- Agency involved:
- Art director and writer responsible for the ad:

So far so normal, but without missing a beat it then went on to ask for:

- Guy in the room at the time:
- Creative director who didn't understand the idea but is now taking all the credit:
- Finance person who said there was no money in awards:

4. "Less is more" was lifted from Robert Browning's 1855 poem "Andrea del Sarto," a poem in the collection *Men and Women*. Browning in turn had taken it from eighteenth-century German poet Christoph Martin Wieland, who credited another German writer, Gotthold Lessing, with its creation.

- Freelancer who said it was all his idea:
- Other creatives who managed to get their name associated with it:
- Account handler whose brief had nothing to do with the final ad:

Its total honesty mocks the proliferation of names that tend to attach themselves to successful ads. As a result, this simple little form stood out and achieved its intended effect with admirable economy.

Irony and sarcasm

Irony: A figure of speech that emphasizes the conflict between the literal and intended meaning of a statement. One thing is said but its opposite is implied.

Sarcasm: A form of wit that deliberately makes its victim the butt of contempt or ridicule.

These two are closely related. The difference is intent: Irony just *is*, whereas sarcasm usually has a purpose. What's more, sarcasm consciously tries to be funny whereas irony usually doesn't (although it might be unintentionally humorous).

Irony is a useful way to create high-impact headlines, especially in situations where it's fine to mock someone's folly. Sarcasm turns up the volume on irony and is effective when you need to talk about something serious, unpleasant, or just plain boring in a way that gets past people's mental defenses.

Irony is notoriously hard to define, although we usually know it when we see it. There's often an amusing inconsistency or incongruity at work, in which an apparently straightforward statement is undercut by its context to suggest a very different meaning. This great little print ad for a Scottish undertakers (created in conjunction with a local health group) does exactly that: "Thank you for smoking."

A paradoxical approach to a serious subject that grabs attention.

DUMB WAYS
to
DIE

Get your TOAST out with a *fork*
Do your own ELECTRICAL *work*
Keep a RATTLESNAKE as a pet
SKATE the platform edge on a *bet*

BE SAFE AROUND TRAINS

Watch the video and download the song
dumbwaystodie.com

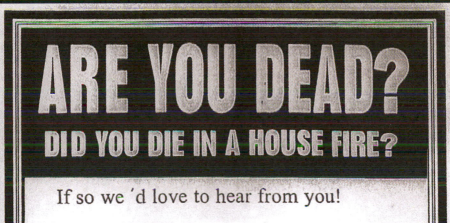

ARE YOU DEAD?

DID YOU DIE IN A HOUSE FIRE?

If so we 'd love to hear from you!

♦ what s it like being burnt to death?

♦ does it hurt?

♦ did you smell like chicken?

♦ the afterlife, where s good?

♦ still got your whatever happens, happens attitude

♦ do you know elvis?

♦ do you regret not spending £5 on a smoke alarm?

helpline: 0800 169 0320

We shouldn't laugh but we do. Sarcasm
for a serious purpose.

There's something deliciously ironic about presenting contemporary tech in such a deliberately dated way. We're not entirely sure what the point is but we like it.

Using nothing more than white text on a black background it raises awareness of the dangers of cigarettes by ironically thanking smokers for their future custom. Similar and equally ironic antismoking ad lines include "For more information on lung cancer, keep smoking" and the brutally no-nonsense "Cancer cures smoking."

In a similar vein, we can't resist this brilliantly written radio ad for Stonewall, the group that campaigns for equality, fairness, and safety on behalf of the non-hetero population. It begins:

Gay son: Mum, Dad, I'm gay.

Dad: YES!!!

Mum: O-my-God, O-my-God, O-my-God, we've got a gay son!! Wait until I tell my sister! She's going to be so jealous.

Dad: I don't want to get my hopes up. You sure you're gay?

Gay son: I'm gay.

Dad: On a scale of one to ten?

Gay Son: Eleven.

Dad: As a tangerine?

Gay son: As a tangerine.

Dad: Yeah! High five!!

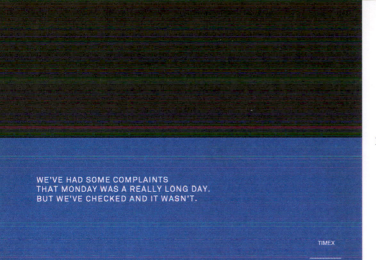

WE'VE HAD SOME COMPLAINTS
THAT MONDAY WAS A REALLY LONG DAY.
BUT WE'VE CHECKED AND IT WASN'T.

TIMEX

OUR RESEARCH SHOWS THAT
THERE ARE, IN FACT, ENOUGH
HOURS IN THE DAY.

TIMEX

OESPITE WHAT YOU MAY HAVE
HEARD. THIS WEEK IS NOT ACTUALLY
GOING REALLY SLOWLY.

TIMEX

Gentle sarcasm that also underscores
Timex's timekeeping expertise.

Before ending:

> Dad: Hey, Reverend Wallis! Didn't see you standing in the porch there. I have a gay son!
>
> Reverend: I heard and I just want you to know that God loves him and the Church accepts him with open arms.
>
> Dad: Sweet!

The final voiceover nails the irony with admirable restraint:

> Until the world is a little more like this, we're here.

Turning to sarcasm, a fine example comes from a press ad run by Scotland's Lothian and Borders Fire Brigade, intended to "encourage" people to fit home smoke alarms (p.153). Deliberately low budget, the result mimics a certain type of market research ad often found in the classified sections of local papers. The banner headline reads, "Are you dead? Did you die in a house fire? If so we'd love to hear from you!" Under which are a series of bullet points:

- What's it like being burnt to death?
- Does it hurt?
- Did you smell like chicken?
- The afterlife, where's good?
- Still got your "whatever happens, happens" attitude?
- Do you know Elvis?

Before ending on:

- Do you regret not spending £5 on a smoke alarm?

By treating this most serious subject in a light-hearted way, the writers poke fun at people who do the same thing at home, highlighting their stupidity and making a memorable message at the same time. The lesson is that sarcasm can be used positively to make a point—all it takes is a little imagination and the confidence to be rude where it counts.

congratulations on spotting that I have learning disabilities. you must be some kind of expert.

Open your mind not your mouth.

ENABLE, 6th floor, 7 Buchanan St, Glasgow G1 3HL. Tel: (0141) 226 4541. Fax: (0141) 204 4398. e-mail: enable@enable.org.uk This poster has been funded by the European Union.

Gee thanks. I never noticed I had learning disabilities until you so kindly pointed it out.

Open your mind not your mouth.

ENABLE, 6th floor, 7 Buchanan St, Glasgow G1 3HL. Tel: (0141) 226 4541. Fax: (0141) 204 4398. e-mail: enable@enable.org.uk This poster has been funded by the European Union.

Justified sarcasm.

Now you have a go

Using the figures of speech described here can take practice. It's
a question of getting your eye in and seeing the potential in your
source material. It's also about giving yourself permission to
have fun with words and explore the outer limits of language.
These exercises should get you started.

Workout One

Number 10 York Street is an ordinary office building in an
extraordinary location, right next door to the iconic 20 York Street
building in central London (the world-famous "Pickle" tower).

As 20 York is only half finished, the owners of 10 York are having
trouble letting their very reasonably priced office space due to the
dirt and noise coming from the huge building site next door.
They've commissioned you to come up with some high-impact
lines to put this right. Your mission is to sell 10 York to prospective
tenants by pointing out its many benefits, and overcoming
objections about dirt and disruption using the techniques
described in this lesson. Your work will be used on billboards,
press ads, and web banners, so each line should be 12 words
or less in length.

To help you, the owners of 10 York provide some background
material. A key point is that, once completed, 20 York will have
a large and very beautiful rooftop garden open to the public. Also,
its ground floor will be very smart and, again, open to everyone,
with cafes, bars, and upmarket stores. *Both are perfect lunchtime
and evening destinations for workers from 10 York.* So tenants of
10 York get all the benefits of 20 York but without the huge rent
bill. Also bear in mind that while it's very noisy today, the
construction phase will end in 18 months.

Workout Two

An engineering company wants to run some trade ads to promote
their new name ("Quantum") and core brand message ("Precision
is everything"). The aim is to announce their new brand and
establish their credentials as suppliers of technically advanced
precision weighing equipment to specialist manufacturing
businesses across Europe.

Your job is to come up with a series of sticky lines that do exactly
that. Use the techniques and figures described in this lesson to
write one or more lines that announce the arrival of Quantum's
new brand and emphasize their excellence. To help you, the big
idea behind their new brand is "smart thinking"—Quantum are
highly intelligent yet down to earth, happy both in the boardroom
and on the factory floor. Try to reflect these qualities in your lines.

Lesson Nine:
Bringing It All Together

Worked examples that put our ideas to work

Combining all the things we've talked about is
the key to really improving your writing.

We've covered a lot of ground, so let's put some of our ideas into practice with three worked examples that focus on writing for digital, brand storytelling, and packaging copy.

We've picked these particular projects, not because they're super-sexy or hyper-slick but because they're the sort of thing brand copywriters do everyday. Nor have we exhaustively explained every choice or decision; by necessity, what follows focuses on just a part of each project. Our aim is to give an insight into an approach, not explain how every sentence came to be.

For the rest of this lesson we'll swap into the first person and let Roger provide a running commentary, as if you were looking over his shoulder. What actually goes on inside someone's head as they tap away is hard —perhaps impossible—to capture. That said, we've tried to describe the writing process as closely as we can, short of sawing the top off Roger's head so you can peek inside (not recommended, either for him or you).

Writing for digital

Despite what they tell you, digital ain't *that* different. When writing for the Web I tend to do everything I do for print, only more so. Online or offline, my readers are the same human beings, motivated by the same things and seeking the same outcomes. It's true that taking advantage of digital to deliver full-on, multichannel experiences requires a different approach, but that's not our focus here.[1]

1. Our point being, we're not here to instruct on search-engine optimization (SEO), content strategy, user-experience design, information architecture, and so on. We have great respect for the talented individuals working in those areas, but what follows restricts itself to the actual process of writing Web copy.

2. That's why this book avoids any discussion of SEO, metrics and analytics, writing for specific social media channels, and so on. Anything we tell you—anything *anyone* tells you—will be out of date in the blink of an eye. We want this book to have lasting relevance and repay your investment for years, so we've steered clear of short-term specifics. If that's wrong we don't want to be right.

There's a school of thought that says writing for digital is a discipline apart, with rules and techniques all its own; we're not so sure. We don't mean that digital isn't important— clearly it's absolutely fundamental to how the world works and will only become more so— but rather that as far as brand-orientated copywriting is concerned, the changes that digital has ushered in are rather less seismic than some commentators would have you believe. Before we're run out of town by an angry mob armed with pitchforks and blazing torches, allow us to explain.

Throughout this book we've emphasized principles over techniques. That's because a principle is long-term while a technique is temporary.[2] By acquiring a solid grasp of the fundamentals you'll be kitted out to create channel-agnostic, media-neutral communications that work equally well on- and offline. Stickiness, stories, audience empathy, figures of speech, and so on are all examples of principle-based advice that will stand you in good stead throughout your career.

That said, we think there are three digital specialisms—information architecture, user-centric design, and content strategy—that any copywriter who chooses to specialize in online comms would do well to know.

Information architecture (or IA) is the science of effective organization. It's about helping audiences find what they're looking for quickly and easily by structuring information in a way that's useful and intuitive. A decent grasp of IA is important for two reasons: It'll enable you to talk on equal terms with others within a digital team/agency, and many of IA's lessons work equally well in the offline world. You don't need to become an expert but you do need to know the main points.

The Allotment
Hello

We're a London-based design and branding business driven by our love for creating brilliant, compelling work that's impossible to ignore. We're obsessed (in a good way) with helping our clients grow. That means finding persuasive big ideas based on 'rich storytelling' that connect with people and help build deeper, more satisfying relationships between people and brands.

To find out how we work please read the six themes below explaining how we can help you grow. They work equally well individually or as a set.

1 / 2 / 3 / 4 / 5 / 6'

To see our latest projects click below or use the main menu.

Our work

Latest work

Awards

UNWRAP A DESIGNER COMPETITION

Latest work

Latest work

Latest news

Latest work

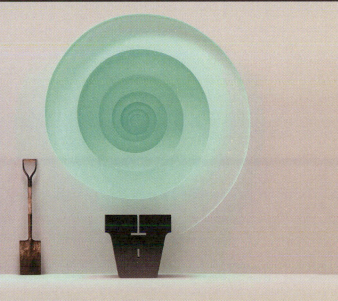

The Allotment
What we do
Our process

1/6 >

Growing understanding

Growing understanding starts with us getting to the heart of the matter. That means digging deep and unearthing everything about your business, markets and audiences as well as the problem you've asked us to solve. In short, growing understanding is about creating a rock-solid strategy on which everything else is built.

*The*Allotment
What we do
Our process

< 2/6 >

Growing clarity

Growing clarity is about finding the single,
exceptional idea that expresses exactly
what's unique about your business or brand.
It's clarifying what you want to be and how
to present yourself to the world. We can't find
this alone. Growing clarity is a collaborative
process that involves working with you to
agree and define your vision. It's about
mapping out exactly where you need to be
heading in order to thrive.

| BrainFood blog | About us | What we do | Our work | Contact us |

---

*The*Allotment
What we do
Our process

< 3/6 >

Growing difference

Having muddied our boots on the big
dig and clarified what makes you unique,
it's time to make you shine. For us this is
critical. Bringing ideas to life in a way that
excites clients and audiences. Our work
is never just eye candy, added on at the
expense of efficacy. Instead, real difference
is achieved through clarity. We build on
what's at the heart of all that you do and
amplify this essence to create something
that stands out; not because it's adorned
with the latest bells and whistles, but
because it's absolutely right.

| BrainFood blog | About us | What we do | Our work | Contact us |

User-centric design is the philosophy and practice of putting humans at the heart of a digital experience. It's a "people first" approach that says the wants and needs of the audience, and not aesthetic or technical considerations, should dictate a website or app's look and feel. The award-winning website for the UK government—www.gov.uk—is a master class in user-centric copywriting and is almost shocking in its clarity and brevity.[3] Orwell would love it.

Another important area is content strategy (or CS). This—you'll be dumbfounded to hear—concerns an organization's strategy for its content; in other words, what they choose to say, and how and where they choose to say it. Sounds familiar? It should, because that's a key concern for all effective copywriting. Having an appropriate, effective content strategy matters for every organization and for every channel—it's just that the offline world doesn't make a song and dance about it.

Our point is that while IA, user-centric design, and CS are important principles within the digital realm, they're important principles in every domain. As we've said elsewhere in this book, it's remarkable how often an idea from one discipline can solve a seemingly intractable problem in another. It's beyond the scope of *Read Me* to delve any deeper into these three fascinating areas, but if you're interested in writing for digital we strongly recommend you familiarize yourself with all three.

---

3. It's been suggested that www.gov.uk's startling lucidity may signal the beginning of the end for tone of voice, in the sense that once other organizations see how well gov.uk's clarity and minimalism work they'll abandon their efforts to create on-page personality and instead embrace an uncompromising "less is more" approach. That doesn't seem too likely to us, but anything that challenges complacency and upsets assumptions has got to be good.

4. Latin filler text, used by designers since at least the 1960s to show where the words should go. Although based on real Latin (written by Cicero, no less) it doesn't have any real meaning. Just so you know.

A website that goes for growth

Today I'm writing a website for a boutique brand-design agency called The Allotment. I've already received an e-mail outlining what the site should say, along with a site map showing all the pages they need, and some rough designs that give me an approximate word count for body copy and headings. My job is to take all this and turn the blocks of placeholder lorem ipsum[4] on the page roughs into something special.

As always, I need to get a good feel for content, audience, and tone. In this case, content is straightforward—it needs to build on the raw material I received in my briefing e-mail. Audience isn't too tricky either—the main people this needs to reach are potential clients. With that in mind, I speak to my contact at The Allotment and we agree the tone needs to be positive, businesslike ,and intelligent, with room for the occasional creative flourish if the subject supports it.

So, content identified, audience clear, tone decided—time to get going.

I begin with the homepage (that's not always the case—often I find it easier to start elsewhere and do the homepage last, once I've got a good idea of what I want to say and how I should be saying it). After a couple of false starts, hammered out with all the finesse of a drunken blacksmith, I arrive at:

> *We're a London-based design and branding business driven by our love for creating brilliant, compelling work that's impossible to ignore.*

It's simple, clear, and direct. The subtle alliteration of b ("branding," "business," "brilliant"), c ("creating," "compelling"), d ("design," "driven"), and i ("impossible," "ignore") sounds gives this version a quiet musicality. I'll go with that for now.

Next I address the idea of growth. I try some wordplay about green fingers and not letting the grass grow under your feet, but it's too much too soon. I realize I'm better off playing it pretty straight at this point:

> *We're obsessed (in a good way) with helping our clients grow. That means finding persuasive big ideas that connect*

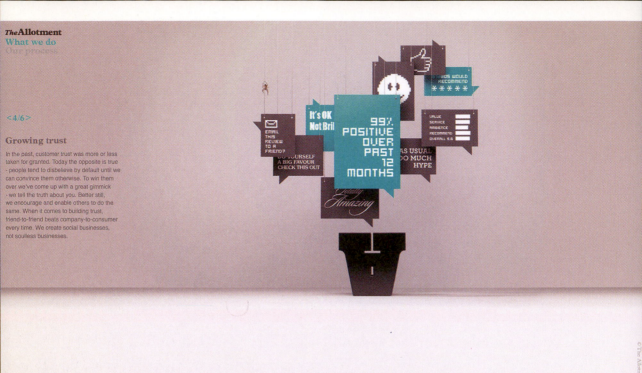

The Allotment
What we do
Our process

<4/6>

Growing trust

In the past, customer trust was more or less taken for granted. Today the opposite is true - people tend to disbelieve by default until we can convince them otherwise. To win them over we've come up with a great gimmick - we tell the truth about you. Better still, we encourage and enable others to do the same. When it comes to building trust, friend-to-friend beats company-to-consumer every time. We create social businesses, not soulless businesses.

| BrainFood blog | About us | What we do | Our work | Contact us |

The Allotment
What we do
Our process

<5/6>

Growing communities

There are millions of social media-enabled conversations happening right now. It's essential that brands with something to say get involved in these conversations themselves. We create compelling reasons for communities to thrive around brands and businesses. We then use our expertise in social and traditional media to create an on going conversation between you and your audience. The point is to give people a reason to believe by presenting what you do in a way that invites - no, demands - attention.

| BrainFood blog | About us | What we do | Our work | Contact us |

Will Awdry

A while ago, some media agency or other announced the average 35-year-old Briton had spent 106 days of their lives watching TV ads. That would mean watching nonstop commercials, 24 hours a day, for *over three months*. Reputedly, an average edition of the *Sunday Times* contains more words than were printed in the entire English language in 1750. In 2012, the number of Facebook users made it the second largest "country" on earth. In the wider online universe, three blogs are started a second, grains of sand joining an already epic beach.

And you want to write for a living?

As the slew of observations above show, there is already too much information in the ether for any attention span to absorb. How can one write with any hope of not getting lost in a pool that deepens by the instant?

In keeping with the power of three, I have a trio of pointers to join the sharp practices already bristling in your quiver.

The first is that, as a representative of a client or brand, your role is to provide informed commentary. Clever observation about your subject is not enough. It's too easy to improvise, displaying your best wordplay, your latest catchphrase, and your most recent gleanings. The danger is you don't bring anything to the party. Good writers know their material inside out, possessing the understanding to make what they have to say interesting. You should too.

The second point is about density. Try to "write light." So many commercials and press ads are compressed to the point of indigestibility. Like a tiny, imploded star, they may be the size of a pumpkin but they weigh the same as Wales. Hopeless. An alternative way of describing the writing in an advertisement is like a dart. You are trying to reach your audience's brain. The right amount of information will balance the flight of the thought and help it find the target. With too many feathers—akin to information overload—the dart crashes onto the floor. No ad can carry every last scrap of knowledge. That's why a copywriter's ability to edit is more critical than the actual writing itself.

A third pointer stems from this way of thinking. Good copywriting is the art of having a conversation with your audience, not cramming them for an exam. More often than not, you're simply gossiping over the garden fence, disguising bullets of commercial salesmanship as a bit of a natter. Obviously this is easy to suggest and hard to pull off. Personally, I still read copy out loud to check whether it's anywhere near engaging. Lecturing is for professors.

Having mentioned these three suggestions, I have reached the stage where experience tells me other people have said it much better than I ever can. "The only end of writing is to enable the reader better to enjoy life or better to endure it," observed Dr. Johnson. Good copy should be useful and entertaining, whatever the medium. Your task is really to use the moments your audience spends with you to help them understand the message. The school prize-day speech one Field Marshal Sir William Robertson gave in 1919 is as succinct an illumination as any on the notion of empathy: "Boys. I have a great deal to say to you but it won't take long: so remember it. Speak the truth. Think of others. Don't dawdle." Equally concise, it's hard to argue with Winston Churchill's counsel as a sort of definitive mantra for any copywriter: "Begin strongly. Have one theme. Use simple language. Leave a picture in the listener's mind. End dramatically."

You're writing to be read or listened to by people who aren't looking out for you. Never forget that. Success means writing well enough to rent space in the synapses of your target audience. Equally importantly, in the mental rental business, you should never go on too long. I know I have.

Will fell into advertising in 1983 and, having risen through various ranks in various agencies, was appointed a creative director of Ogilvy & Mather London in 2008. It's a position he still holds. Throughout his career Will has worked with clients of every shape and size, in both the UK and around the world. He's also won an unfeasible clutch of creative, effectiveness, and craft awards for both himself and—more rewardingly—his teams.

with people and help build deeper, more satisfying relationships.

The main thing the homepage has to do is pique people's interest just enough to get them to keep reading. So in a new paragraph I write:

To find out how we work please read the six themes below explaining how we can help you grow. They work equally well individually or as a set.

OK, that's five sentences totalling 78 words—plenty for the homepage. I'll sleep on what I've just done and instead turn my attention to the six theme pages, all of which build on the idea of growth.

The first needs to focus on how The Allotment can help clients understand the real problem their brand needs to confront. Three sentences should do it:

Note the references to "digging" and "unearthing." I want people to get the whole allotment/garden/growth thing (building on their lovely flowerpot/inverted A logo), so I have to spell it out but without overdoing it. Knowing how far to push a metaphor is never easy but this feels about right.

Next I want to make clear the importance of a single, strong idea and how The Allotment can help clients clarify the thinking behind just such an idea. I decide to tell it straight.

Then it's on to how The Allotment can help clients create difference. The mention of muddy boots is a nod to The Allotment's recurrent theme of all things gardening and growth. It's also an orientation sentence that says, "So far we've talked about X, now let's talk about Y." At 95 words this is the longest page here, but as someone far wiser than I once remarked, "It's not how long you make it, it's how you make it long."

Next I'm onto growing trust. Halfway through I've woven in a reworking of a classic line by Bill Bernbach: "I've got a great gimmick—let's tell the truth," while the last sentence has a nice internal symmetry to it and sums up The Allotment's offer in a memorable way.

After that I look at the theme of communities and, finally, futures.

That's the six main points of The Allotment's offer covered and the backbone of their site in place—let's

call that mission accomplished for now.

I think there are a couple of useful lessons here. When you're writing (or indeed rewriting), perhaps the simplest way to get everything clear in your head is to ask, "How would I say this in speech?" as that's probably how you should say it in writing.

There's also the issue of how far to push a metaphor before it becomes too obvious. There's no hard-and-fast rule; you just need to be sensitive to how the copy feels as it's shaping up onscreen. If in doubt err on the side of caution—overdoing it can seem as though you don't trust the reader to get it.

Finally, when it comes to digital, less really is more—keep your word counts low. Main Web pages containing hundreds of words are just asking to be ignored.

Brand storytelling

We're all suckers for a good story—it's just how we're made. As US author Jonathan Gottschall puts it, "The human mind yields helplessly to the suction of story. No matter how deep we dig in our heels, we just can't resist their gravity." Here's one way to exploit that pull.

A telling tale

I'm writing copy aimed at the marketing and communications teams of large companies. My job is to interest them in specially commissioned social-media research produced by my client Radley Yeldar, one of London's leading communications agencies (hereafter referred to as RY). My copy will be used online and offline in media ranging from a printed brochure to a large and rather prestigious presentation event.

I need a plan, and as always that plan needs to be based on a solid understanding of who my audience are, what they want to hear, and how best to say it.

To get started I listen back to my recording of the briefing session and scribble down the main points I need to cover:

- The last few years have been marred by all manner of scandal and calamities
- Faith in institutions both public and private is at an all-time low
- Social media means savvy businesses can strike up a conversation with stakeholders and rebuild trust
- Despite this, many companies are wary of giving up control of their carefully stage-managed communications
- On the other hand, social media is here to stay and people will use it to discuss their brand whether they like it or not, so…
- Wouldn't it be sensible to make a virtue of necessity and embrace social media?

OK, so far I've built up a decent picture of who I'm speaking to and what I need to say. The question now is how should I say it?

I could play it straight and turn the bulleted list you've just read into prose paragraphs. That would work, but the line of thinking behind my brief is rich and evocative —is there a better way with a bit more appeal?

As I listen back to my recording I hear the project leader suggest I try something based on the theme of superheroes. Hmmm. Given that the report will be called "Release the Power of Social Media," could each of the five main social-media channels it mentions become a different superhero? Indeed they could. And if that's the case, could I use a story to set the scene and create a wave of interest that would carry readers through the rest of the report? Indeed I could.

Armed with an understanding of my audience, my content, and my tone, it's time to get busy.

Superheroes traditionally appear in the hour of greatest need, so my opening line should capture that state of confusion. Thinking about Dark Knights and Caped Crusaders I type:

It was a dark day in Gotham.

Hold on, can't say Gotham—too Batman-specific—so let's make it:

A review of social media communication in the FTSE 100
Research by Radley Yeldar

Release the power of social media

Make the move from storytelling to story sharing

It was a dark day in the city

A shadow settled over the city and seeped into every heart. For too long politicians, corporations and institutions had held sway. And when things went spectacularly, fabulously, astoundingly wrong, trust quietly died. Faith in institutions and corporations sank to an all-time low, and the people – confused, cynical and not a little afraid – were desperate for change.

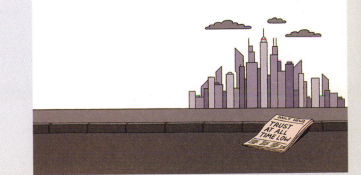

It was a dark day in the city.

Now I need to paint a picture of distrust and desperation. To do this I flesh out the frame of the argument I jotted down earlier. What emerges is an extended metaphor that combines real-world events with the type of situation common to the opening of superhero stories.

If that's not a situation ripe for heroic intervention I don't know what is. It's also instantly recognizable to anyone who hasn't been living in a cave for the last decade (an important point—for an extended metaphor to work, your audience need to recognize what you're talking about). Based on my plan the next paragraph almost writes itself (see right top).

OK, I've set the scene; now I need to spell out the ambivalence, or even antagonism, some businesses feel toward social media. It's not that they dislike these channels per se—they don't; it's simply that Twitter, Facebook and so on give ordinary mortals the power to talk back to corporations and reach a huge audience as they do it. At the time of writing some businesses find this an unsettling prospect. That's where the project leader's comment really comes into its own and the whole approach starts to make sense (see right bottom).

Next I need to make clear that social-media-enabled dialogue has much to offer forward-thinking businesses and that a meeting of minds is in everyone's interests. All the time I'm trying to get my readers to identify with the points raised in the story, something like, "Yes, yes, I'm feeling that, I better keep reading to see what happens." See opposite top left for how I play it:

The next couple of spreads are important, as it's here I make the case for corporations to really embrace social media. By presenting this information in narrative form I can say things in a way that I couldn't quite get away with in prose. My story becomes a sort of Trojan Horse, introducing ideas into the reader's mind almost by stealth. This ability of stories to spell out a truth without seeming to is one of their most powerful properties (see opposite bottom).

An hour later I've filled in the rest of the story by working through my bullets. See opposite far right for how the seventh and final chunk reads:

Out of the shadows

The situation seemed hopeless until out of the shadows emerged a group dedicated to helping citizens find a voice.

Who were they? What was their motive? No one was entirely sure, but that didn't stop them taking these ambassadors of expression to their hearts. And as the news spread, the group moved from the margin to the mainstream. Their power grew, their reputation increased. Ordinary people began to think of them as superheroes with unique powers to provide a platform for everyday people, share ideas and make themselves heard. A ray of light pierced the city's gloom. But not everyone was quite so enthusiastic…

Feeling the fear

Organisations asked, 'Are they superheroes… or supervillains? Just who are these freaks and misfits who dare to dictate terms?'

For big business, the arrival of the caped crusaders spread fear and uncertainty. In the past, businesses had rigorously controlled every message, a situation that suited them well. But now they were being forced to accept a new communications reality, one in which the audience called the shots. The result was a potent mix of dread, disdain and desperation, leaving corporations unsure of how to express themselves.

Meeting the enemy

How could organisations best respond to this unsettling situation?

Some longed to turn back the clock and make these wretched social media superheroes just go away. Ban them, they thought. The more enlightened amongst them knew this was never going to happen, and began asking if they could somehow benefit from the situation. This, they reasoned, was the only realistic option – after all, what we cannot change we must accept. Discussions ensued.

In short, by embracing the potential of social media superheroes to rebuild trust, businesses can enhance their reputation with remarkably little investment. It means relinquishing a little control, but in reality the power to manage the message disappeared long ago – the moment Facebook, Twitter and the other superheroes went live in fact. The new communications reality is about sharing stories, starting a conversation and nurturing audience confidence one step at a time.

A new dawn is upon us…

Accepting the inevitable

Many people are now putting their faith in the social media superheroes, and it's not hard to see why.

Word of mouth carries more weight than a brand's carefully concocted story about itself. Social media offers a hotline to the actual experience of real people. The social media superheroes also give ordinary individuals a voice and allow them to share their views with an almost infinite audience. No wonder they're winning. How should companies respond? The answer is simple: if you can't beat 'em, join 'em. Any business interested in building public trust should seriously consider the benefits of taking the social media superheroes to its heart.

The last sentence contrasts nicely with the first sentence I wrote about a dark day in the city and gives the whole story a pleasing symmetry. With our tale at an end and the readership hopefully engaged it's on to the body of the text—but that's another story.

The lesson here is simple: A narrative can achieve things a straight description can't match. Stories enable writers to show understanding and create empathy without doing so directly. In this case it enabled me to turn each bullet in my skeleton structure into separate installments in an adventure story—an approach that hopefully shouts "Read me!" to any passing eyeballs.

The narrative format also means I can pack plenty of detail into a modest word count. Remember, this is just the introduction to a much longer communication— the detailed research findings and recommendations that follow are considerably straighter in tone. And, as you can see from the accompanying images, the superhero angle gave the illustrators something useful to work with. Holy inspiration, Batman!

Products with built-in personality

Who says a wastebasket has to be boring? With a bit of imagination we can use copy to increase the appeal of the most prosaic item. That's what this job was about.

A kitchen wastebasket with class

I'm working on packaging copy for a new wastebasket. My task is to give it a distinct, appealing personality that will help it stand out in a crowded supermarket hardware aisle. If that sounds dull then think again— to succeed I need to find a quirky, off-center solution that will turn this ordinary object into something extraordinary. When it comes to creativity, your limitations set you free.

The basket already has a working title—OTT—based on the fact that its lid slides over the top of the body, making it easy to empty, and excellent in a tight space.

The designer I'm working with has given me some sketches that explore the idea of turning the upper case letters O, T, and T into an illustrated character, christened—appropriately enough—"Mr. OTT." The sketches look fabulous, so I decide to build on this and bring the character to life. I start by thinking about what Mr. OTT might be like if he were a person. I mess around for a few minutes and arrive at:

Meet Mr. OTT

Mr. OTT is a man of letters. His mission is to make everyday life a little bit better—he doesn't want to change the world, he just wants to change the way we deal with kitchen waste. Mr. OTT believes that by improving even the most humble household item, all domestic life can benefit. So that's exactly what he's busy doing.

I like the idea of Mr. OTT being on a mission to improve everyday existence so I'll stick with this for the time being. It'll never get used in this form (it's a bit like the core-story technique we mentioned back in Lesson Two), but it gives me some useful material that outlines Mr. OTT's personality—slightly eccentric but intelligent and useful.

The brief states we need a tagline. The "man of letters" phrase is cute, given Mr. OTT is literally made of type, but what does it mean? In what sense does Mr. OTT compare to a real-world man of letters (a slightly fusty term for an intellectual)? I try to justify my idea to myself but soon realize the honest answer is "Dunno, it just sounds good," which means I'm guilty of pointless wordplay. Into the wastebasket it goes.

It's always worth checking body copy for potential headlines, taglines, and so on. Reading my paragraph back after dumping "man of letters" I realize that's the case here:

Mr. OTT
Making life a little better

Much improved. It suggests a customer benefit, something "man of letters" didn't do. It's also appealingly modest (in the sense that there's no massive overclaim) and the leading verb makes Mr. OTT an active character (in the sense that he's actually doing something).

Now, he's called OTT so let's see if I can push things a bit. How about some sticky headlines based on the wit and wisdom of Mr. OTT, each of which turns one of the basket's features into a benefit? Throwing caution to the wind I crank out:

> Mr. OTT says: "A good bin is like a sock—good when fresh, bad when it starts to smell."
>
> Mr. OTT says: "Fingerprints belong at a crime scene, not all over my lovely body."
>
> Mr. OTT says: "30 liters should be enough for anyone. If you want more get a dumpster."
>
> Mr. OTT is not at home to hard-to-remove trashbags.
>
> Mr. OTT knows that size matters. Mrs. OTT is delighted with his extra 20%.

They're fun, but are they a bit *too* OTT? Possibly, especially the last. What happens if I bring them back a bit and emphasize the connection with the basket's main features? Here's what:

> A clever seal on my lid means nasty smells can't escape.
>
> I'm coated in a special antifingerprint finish so I stay spotless.
>
> My Over The Top lid means I can swallow 20% more trash.
>
> I'm easy to fill and empty because my lovely lid opens all the way.
>
> I'm designed in the UK by that nice man Nick Munro.

That feels like it's getting somewhere, although I'm still concerned I haven't quite captured the essence of the features I'm trying to explain. Maybe a short subheading for each line would help—a sort of distillation of a distillation:

Fresh thinking

A clever seal on my lid means nasty smells can't escape.

Bright and beautiful

I'm coated in a special antifingerprint finish so I stay spotless.

Think BIG

My Over The Top lid means I can swallow 20% more trash.

Easy does it

I'm easy to fill and empty because my lovely lid opens all the way.

True Brit

I'm designed in the UK by that nice man Nick Munro.

Nice. Notice how each header and copy line is approximately the same length. Graphic designers like that sort of thing—it means they can create a single visual device and then fill it with different text without the need for too much tinkering. Also notice how most of the lines have a regular, parallel structure beginning with "I'm" or "My," suggesting to readers that Mr. OTT is a living, breathing character.

Enough. What have we learned here? I think one lesson is, try to have some fun. Obviously that's not appropriate if you're writing about, say, a new treatment for acute arthritis, but generally speaking, humor is a potent persuader.

Secondly, if you're writing any sort of list or series of points, aim to balance your sentence or phrase lengths—either that or go completely the other way and deliberately reject all equilibrium, just don't sit on the fence. As always, reading what you've written out loud is the best way to reveal its internal rhythm (or lack thereof).

Finally, remember that sometimes you need to do a bit of background writing to get to the foreground stuff. In this case the short "Meet Mr. OTT" paragraph acted as a launchpad for everything else. You don't have to use your first thoughts, but they can help you get to where you need to be.

Lesson Ten:
What You Need to Succeed

The seven habits of highly successful copywriters

PUSH IT

PUSH IT
***REAL* GOOD**

Applied to your career as much as the door.

The previous nine lessons are about how to write copy. As we enter the home straight let's look at how to be a copywriter—in particular, the magnificent seven qualities we think every copywriter needs to give their career a supercharged start.

No one will make your career happen but you. If you want to get on (and the fact you're reading this sentence right now strongly suggests you do), then it's your responsibility to learn all you can, demonstrate your commitment every chance you get, create opportunities where none exist, and generally give Lady Luck a helping hand. As Ogilvy wrote:

If you prefer to spend all your spare time growing roses or playing with your children I like you better, but do not complain that you are not being promoted fast enough.

So that's what this lesson is about—the noble art of Getting On. Over the years we've noticed many of our more successful colleagues share certain well-defined characteristics and work in certain well-defined ways. This similarity suggests they've stumbled onto something important. What follows is a whistle-stop tour through a series of insights it might otherwise take you years to acquire through trial and error.

Habit no. 1—cultivate curiosity

The best copywriters—indeed the best creatives in any field—have an insatiable interest in the world. Many years ago US advertising executive James Webb Young described how the brightest writers he knew were "curious about everything—from Ancient Egyptian burial customs to modern art." We suggest you cultivate the same universal inquisitiveness.

Top of the list of things every writer should be curious about is how good writing works. Luckily that's easy to research—just read more. You'll unconsciously absorb pointers on style, pacing, vocabulary, imagery, storytelling, and the rest, many of which you can make your own. Good prose often employs the "me to you" perspective that we've said is a hallmark of good copy. By reading the right stuff you'll see how a range of authors make and sustain this connection, which is the first step to doing the same yourself.

What should you be reading? Anything from Dostoyevsky to DC Comics—the only real measure is that it works. So-called trash is as valuable as Shakespeare, *provided it's good, effective trash.* If something speaks to you as you read it and its message stays with you once you've finished then it's worth your attention.

opposite: This pastiche, long-copy ad sh[...] a real curiosity for period detail.

Your authors' top ten favorite books (we[...] for today). Roger left, Gyles right.

From a time when...

Ads looked like this. You had big hair. Phillip Schofield had brown hair. Your mum wore shoulder pads. Your dad wore Speedos. You had to fight for your right to party. Losing meant you got a Blankety-Blank cheque book and pen. It was 01 for London.

You came home from school to Zammo McGuire, Gripper Stebson and Ro-land. You held a chicken in the air and stuck a deckchair up your nose. The Sword of Omens gave you sight beyond sight.

You recorded the Top 40 every Sunday, onto a C90 cassette. If you hit 88.8 mph you travelled back in time. Girls just wanted to have fun. Fluorescent colours were the colours to be seen in. Beefy hit the Aussies for six. The Young Ones were young ones.

You drank Slush Puppies in your Hush Puppies. The First Division really was the First Division. You first visited Albert Square, Ramsay Street and Brookside Close. You tried to break dance. You tried to break dance again.

Four TV channels seemed like a lot. You knew never to feed them after midnight and even named your cat after one of them. There was nothing in this game for two in a bed. You couldn't get to sleep without your Glo Worm. Acid rain was a worry. If there was something strange in your neighbourhood, you knew who to call.

You wore leg warmers with everything. Steve Davis made snooker 'interesting'. A crack commando unit was sent to prison by a military court for a crime they didn't commit.

You wondered what would happen if you said 'Beetlejuice' three times. The man from Del Monte, he said "Yes". You wanted to be a Goonie and find One-Eyed Willy's ship. Alex was a steel worker by day, exotic dancer by night. A bunch of bears cared. Kevin Bacon was Footloose.

You practised Ted Rogers' lightning fast 3-2-1 hand gesture in the playground. You were working as a waitress in a cocktail bar. You got, got, got, need, got Panini stickers. Maradona beat England single-handedly. You told the time on your Swatch watch.

A cyborg assassin said he'd be back for the first time. You practised getting in and out of your dad's car through the window, Yee Hah.

Three men struggled to look after one baby. Friendship bracelets were ties that couldn't be broken. You could be his wingman anytime. You tried to catch a fly with chopsticks. Salt and vinegar crisps came in blue packets.

Glenn Close made married men think twice about having an affair. Betamax was cutting edge technology. Michael Knight's best friend was his car. We thought Milli Vanilli were singing. That wasn't a knife, this was a knife.

You played a word association game where you mustn't pause, hesitate, repeat a word or you'd get a bash on the head like this or like this. Sam Fox was a fox. Tom Hanks fell in love with a mermaid.

Hippos were hungry, hungry. Your Hypercolour T-shirt worked brilliantly until your mum washed it for the first time. You would have gotten away with it if it hadn't been for those meddling kids.

Everyone had a poster of a man holding a baby. Crossroads reached the end of the road. You wanted a day off just like Ferris's. Jessica Fletcher helped police find the 'real' killer. You collected Garbage Pail Kids. Aerobies could travel for miles. Louis Winthorpe III and Billy Ray Valentine traded places.

You completed a Rubik's Cube by peeling the stickers off. Dallas was all a dream. Harry met Sally.

Mobile phones were the size of house bricks. Her name was Rio and she was dancing on the sand. Bats were scared of The Prince of Darkness. Jossy Blair managed The Glipton Giants. Ooh, you could crush a grape. Um Bongo, Um Bongo, you drank it in the Congo. Molly Ringwald, Emilio Estevez, Anthony Michael Hall, Judd Nelson and Ally Sheedy were all members of the same club. Luke and Matt made you want to put bottle tops on your shoes.

You asked Bob for a 'P' please. You knew who the Crafty Cockney was. You were going to live forever, you were going to learn how to fly. Floppy records never worked but made great Frisbees.

A piece of folded paper held in your hands could predict someone's future. You were told to say what you saw. You had to watch out, Beadle was about. Sir Clive thought we'd all be driving battery powered tricycles by now.

A material girl was living in a material world. You switched off your TV set and did something less boring instead. Michael Fish assured us there wasn't a hurricane on the way. A Mannequin came to life.

Nick Kamen did his laundry in his boxer shorts. You wanted to shout, shout, let it all out. Gordon the Gopher lived in a broom cupboard. Zippy, George and Bungle shared a house with Geoffrey.

Rick was never gonna give you up. You wanted to make your very own Kelly LeBrock. Romantic men were new and wore their sisters' make-up. Every car seemed to have a Garfield in its window. Torvill and Dean made you want to go ice-skating.

One story was neverending. Eric the schoolboy ate a banana and an amazing transformation occurred. There were halfpennies and one pound notes. You were proud of your picture getting in The Gallery. Computer games took half an hour to load.

You knew all the Ninja Turtles' names and colours. Penny sweets actually cost one penny. We were all Rat fans. Chevy Chase was funny. Lenny Henry was funny. Les Dennis was Les Dennis.

Your BMX had Spokey Dokeys. You wanted to go where everybody knew your name. You walked like an Egyptian. You got free milk at break time.

Greed was good. You had Pac-Man fever. You got bizzy with the fizzy. You had an E.T. lunchbox. Shops weren't open on a Sunday. You could Rentaghost. And Wispa first came out.

Cadbury Wispa. Back from the 80s.

Ben Hughes

I've never liked the term "copywriting," both because it implies that the act of writing copy is somehow different from regular writing (it's not), and because it suggests that the writing itself is what's most important (it's not).

Copywriters, like all writers, have two parts to their job. Part one is figuring out what to say and part two is deciding how best to say it. Early in my career, I was much better at the second part than the first. I wrote beautiful, meaningless sentences that were universally praised for their poetry and universally criticized for lacking any real content. I think this is common among those of us who get into the industry because we love to write. In fact, that's the problem right there—*we love to write*—and while knocking words against each other in an attempt to create sparks is certainly a big chunk of the job, it's not all of it, or even the most crucial part.

First and foremost, copywriting is about ideas, whether it's a brilliantly clear way of explaining a complex subject, a fresh angle on a well-trodden story, an act of synthesis that weaves together seemingly unconnected strands into a sturdy argument, or, quite simply, the truth. It may be a shock to see that last word in there, especially since the general impression of our kind is that we exist to spin bad news or just make things sound pretty, but at its best copywriting uncovers truths that were hidden there all along, in plain sight, and hoists them up for everyone to see.

Some of the best copywriters aren't even very skilled as wordsmiths. They simply come up with astounding ideas and then present them as plainly as possible. A line like Nike's immortal

Olympic reminder that, "You don't win silver, you lose gold," doesn't impress because of its mastery of the subtleties of the English language. It impresses because it gleefully pisses in the face of those sainted athletes who have trained their entire lives only to be second best. Those seven words communicate more about Nike than most brands could get across in a year's worth of work. It's an uncomfortable truth, but it's a truth nonetheless.

You have to build a house before you can decorate it. You may have the perfect painting ready to brighten up the dining room, but without four walls and a roof, there's nowhere to hang it. It's the same with copywriting. Without a strong idea to hang your words on they'll collapse under their own weight, shapeless. Build the house first. You may even find, in the process, that the house is interesting enough on its own without a lot of embellishment cluttering things up.

Don't write copy. Write the truth, write it clearly, and then get out of the way.

Ben Hughes is a writer, creative director, photographer, and filmmaker. His advertising career has included stops at Ogilvy & Mather, R/GA, Mother, and, most recently, Wieden+Kennedy, where he was one of the youngest creative directors in the agency's history. In addition, he has written about music, books, and technology for *Esquire*; directed and edited music videos; created Web content for Le Grand Magistery, *Esquire*, and Little, Brown & Company; and written screenplays for Tribeca Film and Maker Studios. His work has been recognized by the One Show and AICP and nominated for an Emmy. We'd hate him if he wasn't such a thoroughly nice guy.

Of course it's not just books that have something to say—you can learn from anything and anywhere. *If it's got words on it, it's your job to understand how those words work.* Having done so, file away what you have learned for the future. It's amazing how often some tiny feature of a long-forgotten text can suddenly present itself as the perfect solution to a seemingly intractable problem.

What we're saying is, get into the habit of automatically analyzing the words you meet in the world. Immerse yourself in text at every opportunity—how many other professions are there where you can genuinely improve your expertise while appearing to stare vacantly at the label on a beer bottle? As Marcel Proust wrote,

"The real voyage of discovery lies not in seeking new landscapes but in having new eyes."

This is an important point—more or less anything can suggest an idea, it all depends on how you look at it. The more you take in today, the more raw material you'll have to work with tomorrow. Implicit in this is the idea that creativity is about seeing connections, something we'll look at next.

Habit no. 2—seek connections

Connections are the essence of creativity. The best writers, artists, musicians, and so on combine isolated ideas to produce something new that's more than the sum of its parts. It's a 1+1=3 thing.

According to actor, producer, and Monty Python member John Cleese, "Creativity is not a talent. It's a way of operating." And that "way of operating" is about finding connections in order to make something fresh. Back in 1933 Harry Beck, an engineering draftsman by trade, created one of the best infographics ever when he combined the chaotic London Underground system with the clarity of a schematic wiring diagram.

The result was the Tube map that Londoners still use today.

This ability to connect the unconnected is a key skill for copywriters. Work at it long enough and you'll automatically develop the creative "way of operating" described by John Cleese. Seeking—and finding—connections will become second nature; once that happens your creative thinking will come on in leaps and bounds.

Habit no. 3—nurture resilience

Every copywriter needs some iron in the soul. Without inner strength you risk being bruised by the many disappointments you'll encounter in your career. This habit is about finding a way to "keep buggering on" (as Churchill colorfully put it) in the face of all adversity.

To help you, we can't overstate the importance of developing a quiet confidence in your abilities and worth—if you don't believe in you, then why should anyone else? Crass as it sounds, you've *got* to believe you can have great ideas on demand, convert them into magical words, sell them to whoever commissioned you, and generally do your job to a stratospheric standard. If you think you can, you will, so consciously practice self-belief by reminding yourself of your successes, however slight. Everyone is prey to the occasional wobble but if you make a habit of self-doubt then you're lost.

As well as inner strength you also need exterior armor in the form of a rhinolike thick skin. H. G. Wells—author of *The War of the Worlds* and *The Invisible Man*—wrote, "No passion in the world is equal to the passion to alter someone's draft." This urge to tinker is a reliable source of grief for all writers. The only solution is to toughen up so the slings and arrows of

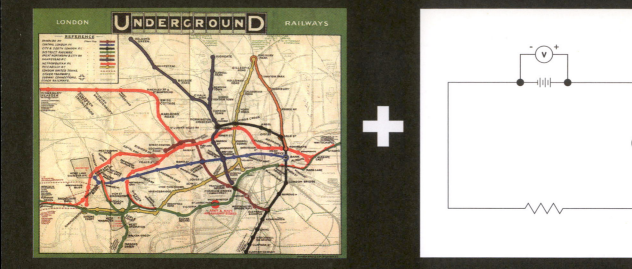

She's my everything went wrong.

For all life's twists and turns:
Flexible financial plans.

 SwissLife

Complicated ideas communicated with ease. A masterclass in making unexpected connections.

I like working with you is impossible.

For all life's twists and turns:
Flexible financial plans.

SwissLife

I never want children are great.

For all life's twists and turns:
Flexible financial plans.

SwissLife

In retrospect Harry Beck's combination of map and circuit diagram seems obvious, but then all great ideas do.

outrageous copy changes don't hurt quite so much (Wells also wrote that "Advertising is legalized lying," but let's move swiftly on).

Annoying though some of these copy changes may be, if they come from someone paying the bill then you must pay attention. Looking on the bright side, they're almost certainly well meaning and might even be beneficial. Back in the day Roger worked at an agency whose boss advised his writers to "assume positive intent" if they were on the receiving end of client criticism. Similarly, Bill Bernbach allegedly went into every client meeting with a typed note in his jacket pocket that read, "They might be right." Both make the same point—like you, the client wants the work to be as good as it possibly can be. The fact they've just rejected all your carefully crafted headlines is simply their strange way of showing it.

Habit no. 4—sell yourself

Most copywriters are in the business of helping brands present their best face to the world. To get into the industry (and get on once you're inside) you need to do the same for yourself. Here's how.

First, your résumé. Visit the websites of established copywriters you admire, download their résumés, and see what features you can borrow—not the words, obviously, but rather any good ideas or layout details. For example, a one-paragraph summary of who you are and what you do right under your name gives interviewers a convenient synopsis/memory-jogging device if they're seeing lots of people over the course of a day.

If you're starting out then you won't have much in the way of experience. Don't try to disguise this. Instead put the most positive spin possible on what you *have* done. Mention absolutely any writing you've produced that could count as copywriting and include any

OCCUPY MADISON AVENUE

NOVEMBER 4TH, 11 AM-295 MADISON

WE THE WORKERS OF THE AMERICAN AD INDUSTRY, PROTEST AGAINST THE FOLLOWING ABUSES, OUTRAGES, AND MALFEASANCES, INCLUDING BUT NOT LIMITED TO:

STAGNANT WAGES *ZERO JOB-SECURITY* *AGEISM* * HOLDING-COMPANY HEGEMONY *STUPID COPY CHANGES*

As if there isn't enough to be angry about.

creative endeavors you've been involved with that show problem-solving and persistence. In the absence of a track record, aim to emphasize the quality of your thinking and your character traits. At this stage it's about communicating your potential.

Next, your portfolio/book. Again, the best advice we can give is look at how others are presenting their work and learn from their approach. Elaborate physical portfolios are probably unnecessary; you'll get far more mileage out of an e-mailable PDF document. Each page needs to include the client name, the agency name, a description of the job format, a summary of what the job was about, and a sample of the choicest text to impress your reader. If the work achieved any useful results then shout them out. Top and tail your PDF portfolio with an intro page at the front (perhaps describing your writing philosophy in a few short lines) and a contact details page at the back.

Next, your website. At a minimum you need a single page that introduces you and prominently features a résumé and portfolio. A good photo never hurts, but for God's sake don't make it inane. If you've got other stuff worth saying then say it, but padding your site is pointless —one lean, mean page is better than six slack ones.

For all these items it's worth investing in some design help. A real designer can make a remarkable difference to even the humblest résumé or portfolio. Do it yourself if you can, but be realistic—if your skills are less than stellar then seek assistance. If you're strapped for cash then find a young designer who needs something writing and swap services—that way you get good-looking promotional material *and* a job you can include in your portfolio.

Finally, let's talk tone. We suggest you keep your résumé and portfolio straight and professional. These are functional documents and not the place to project your personality. You can have a bit more fun with your website but as always, *remember your reader*. They don't want to see anything about your hamster, your holiday, or your love of table hockey. Instead they want to see a quick, intelligent problem solver who's crazy in love with copywriting and who'll be fun to have around the office. Subtly show that your face will fit, and you might get the chance to prove it.

The importance of platform

One way to get yourself noticed is to build and maintain what's sometimes called a platform.

A platform is simply the collective name for the various things you do and the channels you use to tell the world about you and your work. Platforms typically comprise a mix of on- and offline comms, although according to influential US writer Michael Hyatt, they're really built of people in the form of contacts, connections, and followers—whatever tech happens to be involved is incidental and only there to make and sustain connections.

In the online world, blogging is perhaps the most effective way to build a platform. Blog regularly and well about subjects that interest your intended readership, and in time your rep will increase. That's because success today is down to a combination of two things—a compelling product (you), and a compelling way of promoting the product (your platform). Just be aware that nothing will happen overnight and finding an authentic voice (and subject matter) for your blog can take some trial and error. By all means exploit other social-media channels, but the humble blog is probably the best place to begin.

In the offline world, platform building is about doing relevant, interesting stuff. By "stuff" we mean practically anything—from organizing an event to writing a book to making a movie to starting a business. That's because there's real value in side projects that somehow support your wider career goal. Done well, these things can act as a creative crowbar you can use to prise open the door to agencies and get yourself in front of decision makers. They can work as talking points during interviews and as gifts to soften up hard-nosed prospects. They give you a place to try out ideas that might bear fruit in your day job. And they show you're a self-starter who can make stuff happen and who doesn't spend all their spare time watching trash TV.

The point is that while the industry might not be falling over itself to pick you, *you can pick yourself* by making your own way with side projects and personal initiatives that enable you to put your skills into action. As Todd Henry, the chap behind the excellent *Accidental Creative* podcast puts it, "You will be known for what you do, so you better start doing what you want to be known for."

Habit no. 5—work smart

The great microbiologist and chemist Louis Pasteur said, "Chance favors the prepared mind." If you want to capitalize on those rare moments when fate presents you with an opportunity to advance your career then it pays to be prepared, and that means knowing a few tricks about working smarter.

Firstly, you'll struggle to write well if you haven't got inside your subject. While cutting and pasting from source documents is a convenient way to amass raw material, it also means you're not really engaging with what they have to say. Retyping or, better still, writing important material out longhand, creates a far deeper connection. It's the difference between skimming and understanding. And while you're involved in this process of paraphrasing there's a good chance you'll stumble upon a few choice phrases that might make great sticky lines.

Next, we strongly suggest you can explain and justify your work to clients/bosses. As Dave Trott puts it:

"If it's the right thing to do we must be able to explain it. If we can't explain it maybe it isn't the right thing to do."

He goes on to point out that "I like it/don't like it" isn't a reason, it's an opinion. A far better approach is to say "This works/doesn't work because...." Thinking in these terms forces us to introduce a dash of objectivity. Typically that means making some reference to the brief and/or audience. It barely matters what "I" think anyway; it's what they—your readers—think that really counts.

Next, you need to cultivate your listening skills. When you're interviewing someone to root out raw material, remember the old salesman's saying, "you've two ears and one mouth—use 'em in that proportion." However, even the most switched-on listener won't catch everything. It's just not possible to simultaneously take notes, think of the next question, and provide the many reassuring uh-huhs that interviewees need. The solution is a voice recorder or Dictaphone—either a smartphone app or dedicated device. Recording what was actually said means you'll capture every detail. Transcribing it can be tedious, but all that listening and typing concentrates the mind wonderfully and gets you inside the material in a way little else can. We massively recommend the Dictaphone approach.

Lastly, let us praise professionalism. This covers everything from a dogged determination to get the job done regardless of obstacles, through to not stealing from the stationery cupboard. It's all very well being a maverick genius who's on a one-way ticket to immortality and raising hell to get there, but not preparing for meetings, losing important documents, forgetting people's names, avoiding eye contact, leaving the office kitchen looking like a medieval pigsty, texting while talking to clients, and taking a relaxed approach to timekeeping won't win you any friends. So be nice, be sincere, look people in the eye, do tedious stuff with a glad heart, and generally treat your job like, well, a job. People will notice, just as they'll notice the opposite.

Andy York

Most writers I know got into this business by accident, reflecting the diverse group of people we are. I think it strengthens an industry that needs depth and variety. I'm not knocking the many writing courses around; just pointing out that there isn't an approved route or required qualification to be part of this business. Talk to people about how they got started and you'll find no one's the same. And the great thing is there's nothing stopping you.

Having said that, the next thing to say is this isn't about you. If every tone of voice you create—every piece you write—sounds just like you then you're missing the point. All that matters is the voice of the brand.

Every professional writer listens, watches, and reads voraciously. Do the same—way beyond what you write for a living. It gives you a better perspective. There are lines in any soap opera worthy of Pinter at his best. Confront your tastes and comfort zones. Be critical but not prejudiced.

Good writing is good writing wherever it is. Enjoy it. Of course there's rubbish, but *Terminator 4* doesn't make *Terminator 1* a bad film. It just makes *4* a mistake.

We help people sell stuff—however you define selling. We are in business. Be a poet in your spare time (but don't stop writing or reading poetry—it teaches you precision). David Abbott—arguably advertising's best writer—said if your readers are concentrating on your wonderful writing, they're not paying attention to the argument. It's not that I don't like wonderful writing, it's just that brilliance is incidental unless it's what the brand calls for.

Which brings us to murder. Either William Faulkner or Graham Greene said it first, but both were right: "kill your darlings." We've all fallen in love with a fabulous phrase; sometimes we've organized whole pieces around it. It has to go. Kill your darlings.

Biographies of writers are great sources of insights into how to improve your craft. Along with many, many people, I think the best book about writing is *On Writing* by Stephen King. Whether you like his novels or not, can any of us honestly say we have nothing to learn from him? And as you'd expect, it's a great read.

Finally, Cuban crime novelist Leonardo Padura Fuentes gets asked why he still lives in a Havana suburb when his fame means he could live anywhere in the world. The question says a lot about the assumptions of his interviewers.

Padura talks about living in the house his grandfather and father lived in. How essential good coffee is, how important casual conversations on the streets are, and how we balance our perceptions of how life functions around us.

The point he's making is about understanding the context in which you work.

I think that's the first duty we have as writers.

A former Director of Verbal Identity at Interbrand, Andy has worked with some of the world's biggest brands. Today he's a writer and strategist based in London whose clients include The Clearing, OPX, Siegel+Gale, and Fitch. Andy's background in advertising means he's also written for the likes of Leagas Delaney and Publicis. With a foot in both the branding and advertising camps, Andy is just the sort of chap to help readers benefit from his considerable experience.

Habit no. 6—practice pragmatism

"Have no fear of perfection, you'll never reach it." Salvador Dalí

Perfection doesn't exist. Pursuing it is a waste of time and energy that can only end in disappointment. While Writer A is struggling (and inevitably failing) to create a masterpiece by endlessly revising a draft or torturing themselves about whether something works or not, Writer B is just getting on with it.

Lorne Michaels, producer of *Saturday Night Live*, puts it like this, "The show doesn't go out because it's ready; it goes out because it's 11.30." It's a cliché that good enough is good enough, but that's only because it's usually true. We're not saying be satisfied with the first nonsense that flows from your fingertips—clearly you must do the very best you possibly can, but having done that, it's important to acknowledge that getting something reasonably evolved in front of the rest of your team or your client is the best way to make progress. Giving interested parties the opportunity to help develop a piece by suggesting improvements also creates a sense of shared ownership and involvement; that way they'll come to work *for* your idea and not against it.

So our strong advice is this: Get something decent down on paper, make clear it's a first draft, and ask for comments from the project's inner circle. If you're on the right track you'll get a boost to your confidence and the opportunity to address whatever points were raised during this first review; if not then you haven't wasted too much time and you'll have a good idea of how to put things right.

In short, iterative development in public beats quietly killing yourself in private. Remember, this isn't art—no one is expecting a big reveal whereby you pull the dustsheet off your exquisitely wrought masterpiece to gasps of amazement all round. And even if you manage to cook up something you think is perfection itself, the client will inevitably have some comments that disturb the balance of your creation (and possibly your mind). However you look at it, pragmatism eats perfectionism for breakfast.

Roger's reply to a recent graduate asking how to get started as a copywriter:

Dear Nick

Thanks very much for your letter. If you're serious about becoming a copywriter here's what I suggest you do: start learning. Invest in a course or two (only good ones, mind—D&AD and Dark Angels in the UK) and read everything about copywriting you can find (ideally taking notes). The more you know, the better you'll be.

As well as reading about writing it's also a good idea to find one or two heroes and learn from them. There's nothing wrong, and everything right, in apprenticing yourself—formally or informally—to those with more knowledge and experience than you. We learn by copying those we admire. If that means buying the occasional beer or three then so be it. A bar bill today could mean a better career tomorrow.

Then you need to get a toe in the door, and that means approaching agencies. The people to seek out are creative directors. You need to put together a résumé and a portfolio in PDF format of whatever work you think really shows your writing prowess.

It's important you tailor the cover e-mail (which should also be short and appealing) to the agency—look at their website and see if there's anything there you can latch onto—perhaps you've worked in a similar area or know something about one of their clients. You just need a sentence or two to make clear you haven't done a batch mailshot.

Make a list of every agency you can find that employs copywriters and methodically work through, doing say ten applications a week to stop yourself going insane. Offer to do anything; emphasize your tea-making skills and suggest you're just the person to do all the writing work no one else wants to do.

Above all keep at it until you can't stand the rejections any longer, then keep at it some more. And always be aware that a job in a less than perfect company could be a stepping-stone to greater things. I started out as a technical writer for software companies and gradually moved over to creative work through much blood, sweat, and tears. Anyway, good luck and keep in touch. Oh and by the way, it helps to get people's names right. There's no D in "Roger," as my e-mail address makes clear. Just saying.

Cheers

R

Habit no. 7—enjoy it

What they don't tell you at school is that work stinks. Oh sure, you might relish the buzz of getting through the interview process for a few happy months, but the chances are that one day you'll wake up, look at your cheap suit, and think, "What the hell am I doing this for?" OK, you get money, but only in exchange for a large chunk of your life. And you don't get that back.

The good news is that although there are a thousand deathly dull jobs out there, copywriting isn't one of them. It has the potential to be highly rewarding in every sense. On a good day it allows you to combine the best of being a teacher, a journalist, a storyteller, a poet, a carnival barker, a propagandist, a businessman, a psychologist, and any number of other occupations. It allows you to join a motley crew of commercial writers whose history, in one form or another, stretches back to at least the eighteenth century, when Dr. Johnson commented, "Advertisements are now so numerous that…it is necessary to gain attention by magnificence of promises, and by eloquence sometimes sublime and sometimes pathetic."

Successful copywriters are aware of all this. They know things could be a whole lot worse, and whether by luck or judgment (it's usually a bit of both) they've found themselves with a career many people would kill for.

Instead of feeling smug, this knowledge spurs them on to greater things—more hard work, more study, more commitment, more achievement, at which point the process starts again as their status and salary rise.

So give thanks, remember what you've read here, and try to make the next piece of work you do better than anything you've done before. Good luck.

Now you have a go

Ambition shows in everything you do, including sticking at it to the very end. So go on, one last effort before you close the covers and say good riddance to this damn book.

Workout One

You've missed your train. Instead of reaching for your headphones while you wait for the next, have a look around for the nearest piece of copy. It might be an ad, a piece of signage, a public-information statement, or something else entirely—it doesn't matter. What's important is that you cast a critical eye over it and assess what's good and bad about the text. Does it succeed or fail? If it works, how exactly does it achieve its effect? Write a series of bullet points describing and analyzing what you see.

Next, ask yourself what you would change. In other words, how would you rework the copy to either correct any faults or increase its impact? Write out the changes you'd make.

Finally, what can you steal? Is there anything impressive about the text that you feel is worth stashing away for future reference? Write it all down.

Workout Two

Earlier we mentioned the importance of being able to justify your work to colleagues and clients. Thinking about what to say in these situations serves two purposes—it forces you to confront any weakness in your work, and it encourages you to find exciting ways to sell your words (some of which might find their way into the piece itself). Remember, if you don't feel a thrill when you read your words then it's unlikely anyone else will.

To practice this we want you to write a press release for a recent piece of writing you've completed. It should be pithy—three paragraphs are plenty. Describe your work in the most compelling way you can—it doesn't have to be polished, but it does have to be captivating. Your goal is to leave readers desperate to read the piece your press release describes. Our point is that every significant idea you produce should be able to justify the press-release treatment—get that right and you're well on your way to being a star.

Further reading

Some of the following are source material for this book; some are just a really good read.

Paul Arden, *It's Not How Good You Are, It's How Good You Want to Be.* Phaidon Press, 2003

Paul Arden, *Whatever You Think, Think The Opposite.* Penguin, 2006

Marian Bantjes, *I Wonder.* Thames & Hudson, 2011

Pete Barry, *The Advertising Concept Book: Think Now Design Later.* Thames & Hudson, 2012

Jeremy Bullmore, *Behind the Scenes In Advertising (Mark III).* World Advertising Research Centre, 2003

Clive Challis, *Helmut Krone. The Book. Graphic Design and Art Direction (concept, form and meaning) after advertising's Creative Revolution.* The Cambridge Enchorial Press, 2005

Alastair Crompton, *The Craft of Copywriting.* Random House, 1987

The Economist Style Guide. Profile Books, 2005

Alan Fletcher, *The Art of Looking Sideways.* Phaidon Press, 2001

Mark Forster, *Get Everything Done And Still Have Time To Play.* Hodder & Stoughton, 2000

Jonathan Gottschall, *The Storytelling Animal: How Stories Make Us Human.* HMH, 2012

The Guardian Style Guide. Guardian Books, 2007

John Hegarty, *Hegarty on Advertising: Turning Intelligence into Magic.* Thames & Hudson, 2011

Todd Henry, *The Accidental Creative.* Penguin, 2011

Denis Higgins, *The Art of Writing Advertising.* NTC Business Books, 1965

Rian Hughes, *Cult-Ure.* Fiell Publishing, 2010

Teressa Iezzi, *The Idea Writers: Copywriting in a New Media and Marketing Era.* Palgrave Macmillan, 2010

Steven Johnson, *Where Good Ideas Comes From: The Natural History of Innovation.* Penguin Group, 2010

Robert Jones, *The Big Idea.* Harper Collins, 2000

Ralf Langwost, *How to Catch the Big Idea: The Strategies of the Top Creatives.* Publicis Corporate Publishing, 2004

Alfredo Marcantonio, *Well-Written and Red.* Dakini Books, 2003

Alfredo Marcantonio, John O'Driscoll, David Abbott, *Remember Those Great Volkswagen Ads?* Harriman House, 2008

Beryl McAlhone and David Stuart, *A Smile in the Mind.* Phaidon Press, 1998

David Ogilvy, *Confessions of an Advertising Man.* Southbank Publishing, 2011

David Ogilvy, *Ogilvy on Advertising.* Random House, 1998

Wally Olins, *On Brand.* Thames & Hudson, 2004

Mario Pricken, *Creative Advertising: Ideas and Techniques from the World's Best Campaigns.* Thames & Hudson, 2008

Steven Pressfield, *Do the Work.* The Domino Project, 2011

Adrian Shaughnessy, *How To Be A Graphic Designer Without Losing Your Soul.* Laurence King Publishing, 2010

John Simmons, *Dark Angels: How Writing Releases Creativity At Work.* Cyan and Marshall Cavendish, 2006

John Simmons, *The Invisible Grail: How Brands Can Use Words to Engage With Audiences.* Cyan and Marshall Cavendish, 2006

John Simmons, *We, Me, Them and It: How to Write Powerfully for Business.* Cyan and Marshall Cavendish, 2006

John Simmons & Jamie Jauncey, *Room 121:*

A Masterclass in Writing and Communication in Business. Marshall Cavendish, 2011

Luke Sullivan, *Hey Whipple, Squeeze This: The Classic Guide to Creating Great Ads.* John Wiley & Sons, 2012

Dave Trott, *Creative Mischief.* LOAF, 2009

Taschen, any recent D&AD Annual

Taschen, *The Copy Book: How 32 of the World's Best Advertising Writers Write Their Copy.* 2011

Simon Veksner, *How to Make it as an Advertising Creative.* Laurence King Publishing, 2010

James Webb Young, *A Technique for Producing Ideas.* NTC Business Books, 1965

Index

Figures in *italics* refer to illustrations

Picture credits

8, 10t Waterstones brands; Client: Waterstones; Agency: TBWA, London; Copywriter: Nigel Roberts; Art Director: Paul Belford. 10b "A poster should contain no more than eight words.."; Creatives: Tony Strong & Mike Durban; Agency: AMVBBDO. © The Economist Newspaper Limited, London. 11 Shark (Olympus Mju 790 SW); Client: Olympus; Agency: The Red Brick Road, London; Executive Creative Director: Justin Tindall; Marketing Director: Mark Thackara; Copywriter: Dean Webb; Art Director: Matt Allen. 12 Waitrose Cooks' Ingredients labels; Client: Waitrose Ltd; Design Group: Lewis Moberly, London; Design Director: Mary Lewis; Designers: Mary Lewis and Christian Stacey; Copywriters: Mary Lewis, Christian Stacey and Ann Marshall; Typographers: Mary Lewis and Ann Marshall. 13 Design: Innocent Drinks. 14 Colgate Maxfresh—Talk with Confidence; Client: Colgate Palmolive; Agency: Prolam Y&R, Santiago, Chile. 16t Various Artists Holding Page; Creative Directors: Adam Rix and Simon Griffin; Copywriter: Simon Griffin; Designer: Adam Rix; Developer: Jono Brain. 16b Copywriter and Designer: Olly Cooper. 17 Hoxton Street Monster Supplies; Design and copywriting: We Made This; Photographs © alistairhall.co.uk. 18 Red Brick Beer; Beer From Around Here; Client: Red Brick Brewing; Agency: 22squared, Atlanta; Creative Directors: Curt Mueller and John Stapleton; Art Directors: Ryan Hoelting, Josh Robinson, and Isvel Rodriguez; Copywriter: Curt Mueller; Designer: Ryan Hoelting; Illustrators: Ryan Hoelting and Isvel Rodriguez; Photographer: Kyle Burdg; Release time: Summer 2009. 19 Manifesto Manifesto; Copywriter: Kim Mok. 20 Slavery Footprint; Client: Call + Response and the US State Department; Agency and Production Company: MUH·TAY·ZIK | HOF·FER, San Francisco and unit9; Executive Creative Director: John Matejczyk; Creative Director: Diko Daghlian; Copywriters: John Matejczyk, Melissa Blaser, Aaron Sanchez, and Mike Gallucci; Art Directors: Diko Daghlian and Omid Rashidi. 21 Real Crisps; Agency: HarrimanSteel, London; Copywriter: Jo Tanner; Designers: Simon Attfield and Nick Steel. 22 Penguin "Chapters" campaign; Client: Penguin Books, Malaysia; Agency: Y&R Singapore; Creative Director: Rowan Chanen; Copywriter: Edward Ong; Art Director: Kirsten Ackland. 24 The Last Place You Want To Go; Client: Dixons Stores Group; Agency: M&C Saatchi London; Creative Directors: Simon Dicketts and Graham Fink; Copywriter: Simon Dicketts; Art Director: Graham Fink. 26 2010 DM Holiday; Client: Dr Martens; Agency: Opolis Design, Portland; Art Director and Copywriter: Dan Richards. 28 LAGO New Mobility; LAGO S.p.A— Project by Diego Paccagnella. 29 Reproduced by kind permission of Pret A Manger. Photograph © Ambernectar 13: www.flickr.com/photos/16036153@N04/5035764242/ 30 "What are you waiting for?"; Agency: M&C Saatchi, London. 31 © BBH, London. 32 Chain stitching; Client: Howies; Agency: Dye Holloway Murray, London; Creative Director, Writer and Art Director: Dave Dye; Photographer: Laurie Haskell. 33 Millets' "Long List"; Client: Blacks Leisure Group; Agency: Miles Calcraft Briginshaw Duffy, London; Creative team: Emer Stamp & Ben Tollett. 35 Roger Horberry. 36 Big Bang; Client: Rosendorff; Agency: Marketforce, Perth; Copywriter: Tom Wilson; Art Director and Creative Director: Andrew Tinning. 38-39 Barnardo's "Believe in Children"; Photography: Kiran Master. 40 D&AD Workout brochure; Client: D&AD; Concept and design: Radford Wallis; Copywriting: Mandy Wheeler and Radford Wallis. 41 Google Voice Search Mobile App; BBH London. 42 RNIB "You're one of the lucky ones…."; MRM Meteorite, London. 43 "Dear 16-year-old Me"; Evidently. 46, 48 Image Courtesy of The Advertising Archives. 49 Flick My BIC® Special Edition® lighters; Reproduced by kind permission of BIC UK & Ireland. 51 Why Not Associates, London 53t Image Courtesy of The Advertising Archives 53b Reproduced by kind permission of AB InBev UK Limited. 54-55 Squirrel Life; Client: The Royal Parks Foundation; Agency: My Agency, London; Copy: Jason Scott; Design and Art Direction: James Crosby and William Cottam; Creative Director: Luke White. 56 Rolls Royce. 57 Primi Piatti Wine Bottles; Agency: The Jupiter Drawing Room, Cape Town; Creative Director: Joanne Thomas. 58t "Think Small"; Client: Volkswagen; Agency: Doyle Dane Bernbach, New York. Volkswagen Trademarks and advertisement are used with permission of Volkswagen Group of America, Inc. 58b Nike Air "Jordan 1 Newton 0" © NIKE, Inc.; Agency: Simons Palmer Denton Clemmow & Johnson, London; Creative Directors: Chris Palmer and Mark Denton. 59t Marston's Pedigree Ashes; Client: Marston's; Agency: DLKW Lowe, London; Art Director: Richard Prentice; Copywriter: David Adamson; Photographer: Laurie Haskell; Creative Directors: Keith Terry and Jon Elsom; Executive Creative Director: George Prest; Marketing Manager: Des Gallagher. 59b Granny Smiths; Client: Tesco; Advertising Agency: Lowe London; Copywriter: Sam Cartmell; Art Director: Jason Lawes; Photographer: Colin Campbell; Creative Director: Paul Weinberger. 60 Merchants of Attraction; Client: Penhaligon's; Agency: Dye Holloway Murray; Creative Director: Dave Dye; Copywriter: Fran Leach; Art Director: Christopher Bowsher. 61 PDIP website. Client: Paul Dalling, independent proofreader; Design: Wheatcroft&Co; Copywriter: Nick Asbury. 62 Philco widescreen "It's a Whole Different Story" Client: Philco; Agency: Lew'Lara\TBWA, Sao Paulo. 63 Dutch Railways Textbux; DDB° Amsterdam. 64 Costa Coffee—"Alarm Goes Off…"; MRM Meteorite, London. 65 © BMIHT British Motor Industry Heritage Trust. 67 "Strut Like a Fish" © NIKE, Inc.; Client: Nike, ACG;

Agency: Wieden+ Kennedy Amsterdam; Executive Creative Directors: John Norman and Jeff Kling; Copywriter: Brandon Davis; Art Director: Craig Williams; Art Buyer: Andrew Koningen; Project Manager: Sharon Kwiatkowski. 68t VW Blue Motion and DSG; Client: Volkswagen; Agency: DDB London, UK; Creative team: Graham Hall and Hunter Somerville. 68b Waitrose Fresh Herbs; Client: Waitrose Ltd; Design Group: Lewis Moberly, London; Design Director: Mary Lewis; Designer: Poppy Stedman; Copywriter: Mary Lewis; Typographers: Mary Lewis and Ann Marshall. 69 Musica—"Wanna Be a Rock Star"; Agency: The Jupiter Drawing Room, Cape Town; Creative Director: Joanne Thomas. 70 Breakthrough Breast Cancer—"I'm Sorry London"; MRM Meteorite, London. 72 Lurpak Butter; Agency: Wieden+Kennedy London; Creative Directors: Dan Norris and Ray Shaughnessy; Photographer: Nadege Meriau. 74 Mondadori Portfolio via Getty Images. 76 Politics and the English Language by George Orwell (Penguin Classics, 2013). Cover reproduced with permission from Penguin Books. 77 "We Deliver" ADNAMS; Writer and Art Director: David Dye. 78t © NIKE, Inc. 78b Image Courtesy of The Advertising Archives. 80 MUM DAD IOU. Client: Andrew Warner, Expedia; Advertising Agency: Ogilvy & Mather, London; CCO: Gerry Human; Copywriters and Art Directors: Jon Morgan and Mike Watson. 81 Waldo Pancake greeting cards by Jim Smith. 82 Toyota Yaris "It's a Car," reproduced with permission Toyota. 83 TBWA\Chiat\Day. ©Apple Inc. Use with permission. All rights reserved. Apple® and the Apple logo are registered trademark of Apple Inc. 84 BMW X3: World's Longest Banner; Client: Marc Belcourt, BMW Group; Agency: Cundari, Toronto; Chief Creative officer: Brent Choi; Copywriter: Brian Murray; Art Director: Marcella Coad; Associate CD/Art Director: Raul Garcia; Associate Creative Director: Cory Eisentraut; Account Director: Daryn Sutherland; Flash Designer: John Filleti; Account Managers: Katie Lynn and Devon Enright; Developer: Jonathan Lee; Media: Media Experts (Karel Wegert). 86 Erich Auerbach/Getty Images. 88 © Jen Pedler. 90 Hipster Doofus; Client: Urban Eatery, owner Farzad Fre; Agency: Hunt Adkins, Minneapolis; Creative Director / Writer: Doug Adkins; Art Director: Steve Mitchell. 92 "I Want to Make a Horror Movie"; Client: Canal+; Agency: BETC Paris; Global Creative Director: Stéphane Xiberras; Creative Director: Olivier Apers; Art Directors and Copywriters: Gregory Feremback and David Troquier; Graphic Design: Les Graphiquants. 93 "Timberland—Tactical Prints"; Client: Timberland; Agency: Leagas Delaney London; Creative Director: Tim Delaney; Art Director: Chris Clarke; Copywriter: Matt Moreland; Photography: John Ross. 95 Paspaley Polo in the City Series; Client: Polo in the City; Agency: M&C Saatchi Sydney; Writer: Andy Flemming; Art Directors: Michael Jones and Salvator Gullifa; Typographer: Michael Tonello; Creative Director: Ben Welsh. 96 Stannah Print—"If YouThought It Was Hard Leaving Home at 18, Try Doing It at 72" Client: Stannah Stairlifts; Agency: Leagas Delaney London; Creative Director: Rob Burleigh; Art Director: Colin Booth; Copywriter: Ben Stilitz; Photography: Kelvin Murray. 97, 98 "I've Just Split Up" and "I'm Hungover" from the "Create Your Own Collection" campaign; Client: Tate Britain; Agency: Fallon London; Copywriter and Art Director: Juan Cabral. 99 Adopt a New Life; Client: Toronto Humane Society; Agency: Leo Burnett Toronto; Art Directors: Anthony Chelvanathan and Monique Kelley; Copywriter: Steve Persico; Creative Directors: Israel Diaz and Judy John. 102 Morphart Creation/Shutterstock. 105 Attention All Shipping tea towels and oven mitt; written by Roger Horberry, designed by The Workshop for Nick Munro and RNLI. 106 Pastiche Playbill; Client: University of Lincoln, Creative Advertising Degree Show 2009; Art director: Mike Belton and Luke Buxton; Copywriters: Gyles Lingwood and Anys Brown. 107t AP/Press Association Images. 107b Design: Innocent Drinks. 108 Copywriter: John Simmons; Illustrator: Robin Heighway-Bury. Reproduced by kind permission of Diageo. 109 Back to Work—Iron; Client: Honda UK; Agency: Wieden+Kennedy London; Creative Directors: Tony Davidson and Kim Papworth; Art Director: Fabian Berglund; Copywriter: Ida Gronblom; Photographer: David Sykes. 110-111 GRRRR; Client: Honda, UK; Agency: Wieden + Kennedy London; Creative Directors: Tony Davidson & Kim Papworth; Art Directors & Copywriters: Michael Russoff, Sean Thompson, Richard Russell; DIRECTED BY SMITH & FOULKES @ NEXUS PRODUCTIONS. 116, 117 Image Courtesy of The Advertising Archives. 118t Vespa "Our Ride" Print campaign; Client: Piaggio; Agency: Ace Saatchi & Saatchi Manila; Executive Creative Directors: Andrew Petch and Raoul Floresca; Copywriters: Tony Sarmiento and Bogey Bernardo; Art Directors: Biboy Royong and Gelo Lico; Final Artist: Rod Alonzo; Print Producers: Dennis Obien and Rodel Quitain. 118b Specsavers Long Copy "I Saw You on the 16.51 from Finsbury Park to Brixton…"; Creative team: Naomi Bishop, Catherine Thomas, and Xara Higgs at Specsavers Creative. 120 Mercedes Stories in Oil; Client: Mercedes-Benz Trucks; Advertising Agency: BBDO Stuttgart. Copywriters: Wolf-Peter Camphausen, Armin Jochum, Achim Szymanski, and Friedrich Tromm; Art Director: Sebastian Gaissert; Client Marketing Manager: Sascha Thieme. 122 Philip and Karen Smith/Getty Images. 125l Reproduced by kind permission of AB InBev UK Limited. 125r © BMW Group. 126 TBWA\Chiat\Day. ©Apple Inc. Use with permission. All rights reserved. Apple® and the Apple logo are registered trademark of Apple Inc.

128-129 © BBH, London/British Airways. 133 Foundation Querini Stampalia Onlus, Venice. 134 "X" of people; Halifax Bank. 135l Chris Rank/Bloomberg via Getty Images. 135r Rob Wilson/Shutterstock. 138 Joey Boylan/Getty Images. 140t Raising the Roof—Nothing But Potential; Client: Raising The Roof; Agency: Leo Burnett Toronto; Chief Creative Officer: Judy John; Creative Directos: Judy John and Lisa Greenberg; Copywriter: Steve Persico; Art Director: Anthony Chelvanathan; Print Producers: Gladys Bachand and Kim Burchiel; Account Director: Natasha Dagenais; Art Buyer: Leila Courey; Planners: Brent Nelsen and Ian Westworth; Photographer: Anthony Chelvanathan. 140b Reproduced by kind permission of Thomas Erdelyi. 141 Save Troy Library; Leo Burnett Detroit; Writer: Peter McHugh. 142 Run Yourself Ugly Brochure © NIKE, Inc.; Client: Nike Australia; Agency: Publicis Mojo, Australia; Copywriters: Alex Derwin and Darren Spiller; Art Director: Tony Haigh; Creative Director: Darren Spiller; Designer and Typographer: Niels Nolta; Photographer: Adrian Cooke. 143t "Great Minds Like a Think"; Creatives: Tony Strong & Mike Durban; Agency: AMVBBDO. © The Economist Newspaper Limited, London. 143b UHU Glue—Best Use; Agency: Y&R Singapore; Copywriter & Art Director: Ted Royer; Creative Director: Rowan Chanen. 145t I Am; Client: Illamasqua; Agency: Propaganda; Creative Director: Mark Williams; Art Director: Ben Bateson; Copywriter: Simon Griffin; Designer: Craig Hill; Account Director: Natalie Hargreaves. 145b Waterloo Gin ads/posters; Proof Advertising, Austin; Art Director: Rob Story; Writer: Kathy Farley; Typography: Jon Contino; Creative Director: Craig Mikes. 146t "Leader's Digest"; Creative: Aaron Adler; Agency: AMV BBDO. © The Economist Newspaper Limited, London. 146b SNBTS "Crash" and "Broken Waters"; Client: Scottish National Blood Transfusion Service; Agency: The Bridge, Glasgow; Art Director: Simon Parker; Copywriter: Ali Taylor. 147 Stamp; Client: Honda UK; Agency; Wieden+Kennedy London; Creative Directors: Tony Davidson and Kim Papworth; Art Directors: Chris Groom and Sean Thompson; Copywriters: Sean Thompson and Richard Russell; Photographer: Guido Mocafico. 149t Reproduced by kind permission of Bloomsberry & Co. Limited, New Zealand. 149b "Trump Donald"; Team behind the campaign: Agency: Ogilvy & Mather Malaysia/RedCard Singapore; Copywriter: Kenneth Yu; Art Director: Johnnie Tey; Executive Creative Director: Daniel Comar; Client Service: Robert Doswell and David Mayo. 150 Bisto Gravy—Shared Pledge; Client: RHM Foods; Agency: McCann Erickson, London. 152 © Metro Trains Melbourne, Dumb Ways to Die ™. 153 Are You Dead? Client: Lothian and Borders Fire and Rescue Service; Agency: The Union, Edinburgh; Art Director: Gordon Quinn; Copywriter: Adam Smith. 154 Maximidia Seminars; Client: Meio & Mensagem; Agency: Moma Propaganda, Sao Paulo; Creative Director: Rodolfo Sampaio; Copywriter: Adriano Matos; Art Director: Marco Martins; Assistant Art Director: Fernando Lyra; Illustrator: 6b Estúdio; Account Managers: Izabella Vilaça, Luciana Linares, Tomáz Espírito Santo; Approval: Maria Laura Nicotero, Salles Neto, Lilian Calábria. 155 Research; Client: Timex; Agency: Fallon McElligott, London. Copywriter: Andy McLeod; Art director: Richard Flintham. 156 "Expert" and "Gee thanks"; Client: Enable Scotland; Agency: The Union, Edinburgh; Art Director: Ruth Yee; Copywriter: Stuart Anderson. 158 James Brey/Getty Images. 161, 162, 164 Allotment website; The Allotment Brand Design, London; Creative Directors: James Backhurst, Michael Smith, and Paul Middlebrook; Photosonic. 167, 168, 169 Release the power of social media; Reproduced by kind permission of Radley Yeldar, London; Illustrations by Paul Dixon. 170 Mr OTT; Designed by The Workshop for Nick Munro. 172, 174r, Gyles Lingwood. 174l Roger Horberry. 175 Wispa: "From a Time When..."; Client: Cadbury Trebor Bassett; Agency: Publicis London; Copywriters and Art Directors: Alex Ball and Andy Johns; Creative Director: Nik Studzinski. 178tl, 178b © TfL from the London Transport Museum collection. 179 Life's Turns in a Sentence; Client: Swiss Life; Agency: Spillmann/Felser/Leo Burnett, Zurich; Copywriters: Thomas Schöb and Simon Smit; Art Directors: Daniele Barbiero and Reto Clement; Executive Creative Director; Peter Brönnimann.

Roger would like to thank...

... Lucy Wilson, Lotte Horberry, and George Horberry for putting up with me during the writing of this book (and indeed at all other times). Equally praiseworthy are our marvelous contributors (especially John Simmons for his endless encouragement and support over the years), the good people at www.26.org.uk and www.dark-angels.org.uk, Richard Palmer and everyone at theWorkshop (especially Andrew Turner for Mr. OTT and Michael Batey for his insightful review comments), Carl Radley and everyone at Radley Yeldar (especially Andrew Gorman and Richard Coope), James Backhurst and everyone at The Allotment, and Elliott Starr for his thoughts on the life and death of long copy. A tip o' the hat to one and all.

About Roger Horberry

Roger writes: My copywriting career began at 9.00am on 13 August 1990. Since then I've written about everything from finance and fireworks to telecoms and teabags, producing ads, brochures, websites, presentations, packaging, and brand personalities along the way for clients big and small. My work has appeared in the *D&AD Annual* and the *Creative Review* and Design Week Awards on several occasions. As well as actual writing I also run copy workshops and guest lecture at the University of Lincoln and elsewhere. I've published three previous books: *Brilliant Copywriting*, *Sounds Good on Paper*, and *100 Lessons on the Meaning of Life*.

Roger blogs at www.rogerhorberry.com. E-mail him at roger@rogerhorberry.com or follow him at @rogerhorberry.

Gyles would like to thank...

... my incredibly supportive wife, Kathleen, and our two wonderful two sons, Oscar and George. Huge thanks must go to the students, graduates, and staff team on the Creative Advertising course at the University of Lincoln, particularly Mike Belton and Justin Tagg. Thank you to everyone at Laurence King, particularly Jo Lightfoot, Susan George, Peter Jones, and our picture researcher Raffaella Morini. And of course, a huge thank you to all our contributors, namely John Simmons, Chris Waite, Andi Teran, Nick Law, Stephen Leslie, Simon Veksner, Ben Kay, Wendy Ide, Lucy Sweet, Iain Aitch, David Sandhu, Kim Mok, Mandy Wheeler, Luke Sullivan, Will Awdry, Ben Hughes, and Andy York.

About Gyles Lingwood

Gyles Lingwood is Principal Lecturer at the Lincoln School of Art & Design at the University of Lincoln, where he created the highly regarded Creative Advertising degree course. After graduating from the Birmingham Institute of Art & Design he worked in central London for a variety of advertising and design companies. Gyles's work has been featured in the national design press and has won a number of awards from, among others, D&AD, the British Interactive Media Association, and the US Creativity Awards. His students are regularly successful in national and international advertising competitions, including D&AD and YCN. He has a distinction in MA Design: Visual Communication, has been on validation panels for UK higher-education advertising courses, and regularly undertakes advisory roles in the area of creative advertising and design education. Write to him at gyles.lingwood@gmail.com<mailto:gyles.lingwood@gmail.com> or follow him on Twitter: @gyleslingwood.